BEING A LIVING PRAISE

RICKY CLEMONS

PUBLISHED BY FIDELI PUBLISHING, INC.

ISBN: 978-1-955622-24-0

Published by

Fideli Publishing, Inc.
119 W. Morgan St.
Martinsville, IN 46151
www.FideliPublishing.com

Table of Contents

Being a Living Praise

We should be a living praise unto the Lord Jesus Christ every day, because people need to see a living praise in our body language.

Praises unto the Lord are not only voicing our praises, because that is not enough to convince people to believe.

Voicing our praises unto the Lord is only a small thing compared to praising the Lord with our actions that people will see and know that we are praising the Lord.

Being a living praise is to share our spiritual gifts with one another.

Being a living praise is to help one another.

Being a living praise is to feed the hungry.

Being a living praise is to help the needy.

Being a living praise is to visit the widows.

Being a living praise is to visit the orphans.

Being a living praise is to return faithful tithes and offerings unto the Lord.

Being a living praise is to love everybody.

Praising the Lord only in words is not enough to have a good influence on people who want to change from their wicked ways.

Being a living praise can surely convince people to want to change and live for the Lord.

I can write all of the praise poetry that I want, but if I am not a living praise then all of my writing is in vain.

Being a living praise is to live right unto the Lord, regardless of the trials we have in our lives.

Being a living praise is loving everyone, even our enemies.

Being a living praise is treating everybody right.

Being a living praise is to live the truth of God's holy word.

Praises unto the Lord in our body language will surely cause the devil to flee from us.

Praising the Lord in our body language can surely convince people to believe that we are children of God.

Praising the Lord in words is always good to do.

Praising the Lord in our actions will surely reveal to the people of the world that we are holy and righteous people in the Lord.

Many people say that actions speak louder than words.

When Jesus Christ lived in this world without sin, He was the greatest living praise to God before many people who were so amazed when Jesus spoke to them.

They were also even more moved with convictions and conversion by seeing Jesus being a living praise with His perfect body language in His every action, which was more convincing to people than His words.

Being a living praise unto the Lord is acting out a Christian life beyond our words of Christianity.

Being a living praise is to live right by example before people.

Words of praise unto the Lord can change into negativity when things are going badly in our lives.

Being a living praise is trusting and waiting on the Lord to work the bad things out for our good.

We All Fall Short
of the Glory of God

We all will not say the right words all of the time.

None of us is word perfect.

We can get angry and say something wrong.

We can feel really tired and say something wrong.

We all fall short of the glory of God.

We can get very excited and say something wrong.

We can get discouraged and say something wrong.

We can get confused and say something wrong.

We all fall short of the glory of God.

We can get impatient and say something wrong.

We all won't do everything right all the time.

We can get angry and do something wrong.

We can get confused and do something wrong.

We can get discouraged and do something wrong.

We can get impatient and do something wrong.

We can get anxious and do something wrong.

None of us are perfect in our actions.

We all fall short of the glory of God.

The most educated people in this world are not perfect to have sins.

The most famous people in this world are not perfect to have sins.

The most skillful people in this world are not perfect to have sins.

We all fall short of the glory of God.

The most beautiful people in this world are not perfect to have sins.

The richest people in this world are not perfect to have sins.

The hardest-working people in this world are not perfect to have sins.

We all fall short of the glory of God.

The friendliest people in this world are not perfect to have sins.

We all fall short of the glory of God.

The wisest people in this world are not perfect to have sins.

The bravest people in this world are not perfect to have sins.

The most faithful and obedient Christians in this world are not perfect to have sins to confess and repent unto the Lord Jesus Christ.

We all fall short of the glory of God, but we all can choose to believe in Jesus Christ and be saved from our sins.

Only Jesus never fell short of the glory of God because Jesus was without sin when He lived here in the sinful world with sinners like you and me.

In This World Together

We all are in this world together, whether we are good or bad or happy or sad.

We all have so much in common.

We all need to eat food and we all need to drink water.

We all need to get some sleep and we all need to bathe.

We all are in this world together, whether we are rich or poor.

We all need air to breathe and we all need the sunlight shining down on us.

We all have talents and we all have feelings.

We all have a mind and we all have a heart.

We all have so much in common because we all are in this world together.

We all are in this world together whether we are educated or not educated.

We all are in this world together whether we are wise or foolish.

We all are in this world together whether we are well or sick.

We all need the Lord and we all have a free will.

We all were born in sin.

We all need a Savior.

We all can be saved.

We all are in this world together whether we are introverted or extroverted.

We all are in this world together whether we are white, black, brown, red, or yellow.

We all are human beings.

We all have red blood.

We all have one body.

We all are in this world together whether we have peace or war.

We all live here on earth.

We all can cough and we all can sneeze.

We all can dream.

We all can hope.

We all can get disappointed.

We all can be encouraged.

We all can get sick.

We all can die.

We all can get weak.

We all are in this world together whether we are a Christian or an atheist.

We all can have a good or bad influence on one another.

We all need some help sometimes.

We all don't know everything.

We all make mistakes.

We all have flaws.

We all have habits.

We all have senses.

We all have a soul.

We all are in this world together whether we love or hate one another.

We all are in this world together whether we bless one another or curse one another.

We all are in this world together whether we love Jesus or love living in sin.

We all are sinners saved through grace.

We all are lost without Jesus Christ, who gave up His life on the cross to save us from our sins.

We all are in this world together whether we go to heaven or hell.

We all are in this world to live, whether we go to heaven or go to hell.

We all are in this world together to live, whether we do wrong and shorten our lives or do what is right to prolong our lives.

We all have a destiny.

We all can learn something from one another.

We all can pray to God.

We all can confess our sins and repent.

We all are in this world together, whether we are sane or insane.

We all fall short of God's glory.

We all belong to God.

We all are in this world together, whether we are male or female.

We all are in this world together, whether we are straight, gay, lesbian or transgender.

We all need love.

We all need to love God in order to love everybody in this world.

We all are in this world together, whether we are normal or abnormal.

We all have an IQ.

We all are in this world together to live right by God, who won't force anyone to live right but we all will regret it if we don't live right by God.

We all are in this world together, whether we prosper or don't prosper.

We all are in this world together, whether we are free or a slave to something.

We all are in this world together to be a slave to Jesus Christ or a slave to the devil, but being a slave to Jesus Christ is true freedom from living in the enslavement of sin.

We all are in this world together, whether we know what is right or don't know what is right.

We all are in this world together, whether we tell the truth or tell lies.

We all are in this world together, whether we are confident or not confident.

We all are wonderfully made by our creator, God, regardless of our differences.

We Can't Judge People

We can't judge people, but we know that it's wrong to kill someone.

We don't know people's motives in their hearts, but what people do comes from their hearts whether it's good or evil deeds.

We can't judge people, but we know if someone says curse words it doesn't sound good because it's not good to curse.

We can't judge people, but speaking the truth to people about what they are doing wrong is not judging them.

A lot of people will believe that speaking the truth is judgment, but the truth is proof of people being guilty of their wrongdoings.

We can't judge people, but we have sense enough to know that it's wrong to treat people bad.

We don't know people's intentions in their hearts, but what people say and do comes from their hearts.

When we hear people talking negative and doing something wrong, we have sense enough to know that it's not right.

We can't judge people, but we can speak the truth about people doing evil things and that is not a judgmental statement.

We can't judge people, but when we see people speeding on the road we know that a police officer will give those people a speeding ticket.

We can't judge people in this life, but one day we will judge the fallen angels and all the wicked dead people while we live in heaven for a thousand years.

We can't judge people, but wrong is wrong no matter who does the wrong.

The judges in the court rooms can't judge people's motives in their hearts, but the judges can sentence people to prison for committing crimes through their bad actions that are wrong doings.

We can't judge people, but doing what's right and fair can keep people out of trouble, while doing what's wrong can be troublesome anywhere and anytime.

Only the Lord God Jesus Christ can judge us all right now, but if we make it to heaven we will judge the fallen angels and all of the wicked people who will be cast into the lake of fire and brimstone.

Are Like Twin Brothers

The truth and a lie are like twin brothers who look so much alike.

Many people will believe the truth to be a lie.

Many people will believe a lie to be the truth.

A lie can sound so much like the truth.

A lie loves to imitate the truth, but the truth will never imitate a lie.

The truth and a lie are like twin brothers who can talk so much alike.

You can tell many people the truth, but they may believe it to be a lie.

You can tell many people a lie, and they may believe it to be the truth.

The truth and a lie are so close together that you can't always tell them apart.

The best way that you and I can know the difference between the truth and a lie is to read God's holy word, because that is all truth.

The truth and lie are like twin brothers who can dress alike so that you and I cannot tell them apart from each other.

The truth and a lie can be so much alike because the truth can cause us to feel good just like a lie can cause us to feel good.

The truth will look like a lie to many people, and a lie will look like the truth to many people.

In the garden of Eden, the devil's lies seemed like the truth.

Jesus Christ was the living truth in the presence of the Pharisees, who believe that Jesus was a liar when He claimed to be the son of God in their presence.

The truth and a lie are like twin brothers who can talk so much alike, but the truth's breath will never smell bad.

The truth and a lie can act so much alike, but the truth will never pretend.

Even a liar can pass a lie detector test and look like he or she is telling the truth, but God sees every lie being far from the truth.

The truth and a lie are like twin brothers, and only God will always know the difference.

It's Like Trying to Put Ourselves Above God

If we don't forgive others for doing us wrong, it's like trying to put ourselves above God who will forgive us of our sins if we confess and repent of our sins.

What if God didn't forgive us when we did God wrong in ways that we didn't realize?

We would be better off never being born if God didn't forgive us of our sins.

Who are we to believe that we are too good to not forgive others, who God will forgive if they confess and repent of their sins?

No matter what wrong thing someone does to us, God will sooner or later get vengeance that can surely cause that someone to straighten up and do right by Him.

If you and I seek revenge when someone does us wrong, it's like trying to put ourselves above God, whose vengeance is always good to save a soul from being lost, when our vengeance can surely cause a soul to be more lost in sin.

We know that it is not easy to forgive when someone does us wrong, but who are we to believe that we are better than those who hurt us?

We hurt God if we don't forgive others who He also loves and gave His son, Jesus Christ, to save them from their sins.

It's like trying to put ourselves above God if we don't forgive someone for doing us wrong.

That someone may make it to heaven someday, but we will go to hell for having an unforgiving heart that displeases God.

If you and I don't forgive someone for doing us wrong, it won't stop God from forgiving him or her because they may not know that they have done us wrong.

It's like trying to put ourselves above God if we hold onto grudges and don't forgive others.

You and I do God wrong every day in some kind of way, unseen or seen, and God has every right to not forgive us for this.

But God is forevermore better than us.

Forgiving others will set us free from hurting people and the wrong they do us won't have a lasting bad effect on us.

Who are we to not forgive oneself who God will forgive because God loves us even if we don't love oneself.

Predestined

Nobody is predestined to be saved and nobody is predestined to be lost.

The Lord has given everyone the free will to choose to be saved or be lost.

If we were predestined to be saved, then we could live our lives any kind of way and break God's law like it doesn't exist at all.

We could live a rebellious life and still be saved and go to heaven if we were predestined to be saved.

If we were predestined to be lost, then what's the use in going to church to worship the Lord?

Jesus Christ would have had no need to give up His life on the cross for us if we were predestined to go to hell.

We choose our own destiny that will come to us when we have no predestined fate that tells whether we will live right unto the Lord or live for the devil.

Our choices determine where we will end up.

If we were predestined to be saved, then Jesus would have had no need to even have been born into this world where He had to come to save us from our sins.

If we were predestined to be lost, then Jesus would have no need to represent our case before God in heaven.

Even Lucifer was not predestined to rebel against God.

Lucifer had to choose to rebel and meet his fate in hell one day.

If we were predestined to be lost in hell, then Jesus Christ would not have left heaven to live in a world among sinners.

The only predestined thing that we can claim is that we all were predestined to have a free will.

God predestined us all to have a free will because God does not force anyone to love and obey Him.

It Sounds Good
But It's Not True

It sounds good when people say that we go to heaven right after we die, but that is not true.

The Bible says that Jesus Christ is coming back again to take us to heaven when we die.

When we die, our spirit goes back to God, while our body stays in the grave.

Our spirit is the breath that we breathe.

It sounds good when people say that we go to heaven right after we die.

Jesus Christ would have no need to come back again on the clouds of glory if there was no one in the grave for him to raise from the dead.

The Bible says the Jesus will raise the righteousness dead and change the righteous living from mortal to immortal in the twinkling of an eye.

Now, that sounds good and it is true that Jesus will take us to heaven when He comes back again.

None of our dead loved ones are looking down on us from heaven.

They are in the grave waiting on Jesus Christ to come back again and raise them from the dead.

Jesus will put their breath back in their bodies so they can live again without sin if they died being saved in Him.

The fallen angels will appear to be our dead loved ones and talking to us from heaven.

The angels from heaven will never appear to be our dead loved ones, but they will appear unaware to us and we will not know who they are.

Many preachers will say when we die we go to heaven right after we die, but it's not true.

The Lord will hold him accountable for speaking that lie and not being in line with God's holy word.

Our Life is an Open Book

Our life is an open book to read for as long as we live.

Our actions can be read so clearly sometimes, just like an open book that we can read every day.

Some people can read our eyes and see love or hate in them.

Some people can read the tips of our tongues and understand the words that we say.

Some people can read our minds and know what we will say and do.

Our lives are an open book that some people can read very well.

You can fool some people, but you can't fool everybody and still be an open book to read.

Our lives are an open book to the angels in heaven who will put a comma on our lives.

Our lives are an open book to the fallen angel who will try to scramble up the paragraphs in our lives so that we are incorrect to one another.

Our lives are an open book to Jesus, who loves to correct the punctuation in our lives and the misspelled words in our lives.

Jesus is happy to do this for us if we love Him and keep His Commandments.

Our lives are an open book that death loves to close and put up on the shelf of no returns so that they collect the dust of the grave.

Jesus Christ is the open book of eternal life that death can never close for you and me.

For us to read our way into heaven, we must be saved in Jesus Christ.

Today we can read about Jesus' life in the Bible, where His life is an open book that many people close because they don't read the Bible every day.

Our lives are an open book and we are the authors of our choices in life.

Jesus is our publisher and book printing company who distributes us to eternity if we are saved in Him.

To the Lord Than

A dull song unto the Lord is greater to the Lord than the most beautiful worldly love songs.

A broken prayer from the heart unto the Lord is greater to the Lord than a polished-up prayer from the head.

The smallest works unto the Lord are greater to the Lord than the most brilliant works of the world.

The simplest words about the Lord are greater to the Lord than the most intellectual words of the world.

The smallest works unto the Lord are bigger to the Lord than the most dedicated deeds of the world.

A modest appeal unto the Lord is more beautiful to the Lord than the most beautiful fashions of the world.

A dull sermon about the Lord is more powerful to the Lord than the greatest speeches of the world.

A boring Sabbath school lesson is more interesting to the Lord than the greatest lectures of the world.

Going to church to worship the Lord is greater to the Lord than traveling around the world to see the wonders in this world that belong to the Lord.

The smallest faith in the Lord is more visible to the Lord than the biggest visible things in this world.

Living our lives unto the Lord is more precious to the Lord than all the world's luxury living in the past, present and future.

Without Jesus in Our Lives

Without Jesus in our lives, we are like a lost memory that we won't get back.

Without Jesus in our lives, we are like a wanderer who doesn't know where he's going.

Without Jesus in our lives, we are like the invisible wind that it has no substance.

Without Jesus in our lives, we are like a falling star, disappearing out of sight.

Without Jesus in our lives, we are like walking in our sleep as though we are awake.

Without Jesus in our lives, we are like an illusion that is not real.

Without Jesus in our lives, we are like the unknown that hides its presence from us.

Without Jesus in our lives, we are like a dream that reality can crush.

Without Jesus in our lives, we are like smoke that can suffocate in any living creature.

Without Jesus in our lives, we are like a poisonous snake that will strike at anyone or anything that moves near to it.

We Live in a World

We live in a world where many people believe that good is evil and evil is good.

We live in a world where many people believe that right is wrong and wrong is right.

We live in a world where many people believe that a man should be with a man and a woman should be with a woman.

We live in a world where many people believe that it's right to hate.

We live in a world where many people believe that it's good to tell lies.

We live in a world where many people believe it's right to kill.

We live in a world where many people believe that it's right to steal.

We live in a world where many people believe that it's right to be unfaithful.

We live in a world where many people believe that there is no God.

We live in a world where many people believe that the church is boring.

We live in a world where many people believe that the innocent are guilty and the guilty are innocent.

We live in a world where many people believe that a criminal is good.

We live in a world where many people believe that a lie is the truth and the truth is a lie.

We live in a world where many people believe that being kind is weak and being mean is strong.

We live in a world where many people believe that talking a lot is being smart and being quiet is being stupid.

We live in a world where many people believe that Christians are bad.

We live in a world where many people believe that foolishness is good.

We live in a world where many people believe that the Bible is a fairytale book.

We live in a world where many people believe that there is no devil.

We live in a world where many people believe that money can solve all of their problems and they believe that Jesus Christ can do nothing for them.

Prejudice is Nothing New Today

Prejudice is nothing new today

Prejudice began up in heaven where Lucifer disliked God for ruling over him.

Lucifer disliked God for not allowing him to be in on the creation of the heavens and earth.

Cain was prejudiced against his brother Abel because Abel gave a better sacrifice to God.

Cain believed that he was better than Abel and that God should have accepted his sacrifice over Abel's sacrifice.

Many Egyptians were prejudiced against the Hebrews and put them into slavery because they were threatened by the vast number of Hebrews.

King pharaoh was afraid of the Hebrews in Egypt and thought they would take his kingdom from him.

King pharaoh disliked the Hebrews for prospering in his kingdom.

Many Jews were prejudiced against the Samaritans because they were a mixed breed of people who didn't look like them.

Back in the Bible days, many of the Jews were prejudiced against the Gentiles and believed they were better than the Gentiles because the Gentiles were not circumcised.

The Jews believed that the Gentiles had to be circumcised to be saved.

Prejudice is nothing new, and it's seen a lot more around the world today.

Prejudice is of the devil, who has his human agents who dislike people if they look different from them.

There will be no prejudice in the new heaven and new earth where there will be nothing but love with no dislikes.

When Things are Going Good

When things are going good in my life, I still need you, O Lord.

I truly thank you, O Lord, for allowing good things to go on in my life as if I have no trials in my life.

When things are going good in my life, it's no time for me to get slack in my prayers unto you, my Lord.

When things are going good in my life, it's no time for me to get slack in reading the Bible.

When things are going good in my life, it's no time for me to get slack in loving and obeying You, my Lord and Savior, Jesus Christ.

O Lord, you are so good to me, even when things are not going good in my life.

O Lord, you never promised me that the road would always be easy to walk through my life.

When things are going good in my life, it's no time for me to get slack in using my spiritual gift to uplift the church.

When things are going good in my life, it's no time for me to get slack in being a witness of You, my Lord Jesus Christ.

When things are going good in my life, it's no time for me to get slack in loving my brothers and sisters in the church.

When things are going good in my life, it's no time for me to get slack in giving You the glory and praise, my Lord Jesus Christ.

When things are going good in my life, it's because of you, my Lord, who I can always trust even when things are not going good.

I know this because it's never too hard for You to move things out of my way in Your time, and You are always on time.

When things are going good in my life, and when things are going bad in my life, it's Your will, O Lord, for my life and not my will that is flawed for me to get slack in humility onto you, my Lord.

Poets are Like an Umbrella

Poets are like an umbrella that we need to use to cover us when the rain falls in life.

There are many poets who write and recite praise poetry, prose poetry, rhyming poetry, sonic poetry, concrete poetry, phrases poetry, eulogy poetry, haiku poetry, epic poetry, limerick poetry, and abecedarian poetry.

Poets are like an umbrella covering our brokenness in this broken world.

An umbrella can surely protect us from getting wet in the rain.

An umbrella can surely protect us from the hot, scorching sun.

Poets are like an umbrella protecting us from the heavy rainfall of doom.

Poets are like an umbrella protecting us from the hot, scorching sun of mental and emotional strain.

There are poets who don't write and recite poetry about the Lord Jesus Christ, but they are still like an umbrella to cover over and protect many people from the icy hail of discouragement.

In the book of Psalm, King David was also a poet who covers over you and me like an umbrella when we read the book of Psalm where King David had his ups and downs in life.

Poets are like an umbrella that can get all wet with dripping rain drops, but you and I are kept dry and comfortable.

We Christian poets are like an umbrella to especially get all wet up in the heavy rainfall of worldly people and doubtfulness about the Lord.

Christian poets are like an umbrella to especially get all wet up in the heavy rainfall of unrepentant souls while covering over their cold hearts and delusional minds that they have for not believing in Jesus Christ, who Christian poets believe in and love and obey.

O Lord, You Will Always

O Lord, you will always understand me.

O Lord, you will always talk to me.

O Lord, you will always listen to me.

O Lord, you will always help me.

O Lord, you will always come for me.

O Lord, you will always encourage me.

O Lord, you will always motivate me.

O Lord, you will always strengthen me.

O Lord, you will always be there for me.

O Lord, you will always stand by me.

O Lord, you will always give me peace of mind.

O Lord, you will always lift me up.

O Lord, you will always be good to me.

O Lord, you will always give me joy.

O Lord, you will always protect me.

O Lord, you will always correct me.

O Lord, you will always treat me right.

O Lord, you will always be fair to me.

O Lord, you will always fight my battles.

O Lord, you will always give me the victory.

O Lord, you will always lighten my burdens.

O Lord, you always tell me the truth.

O Lord, you will always warn me not to do evil.

O Lord, you will always let me choose to live for You or live for the devil.

O Lord, you will always let me choose life or death.

O Lord, you will always let me choose my destiny.

O Lord, you will always be a friend to me.

O Lord, you will always give me what I need.

O Lord, you will always let me know when something is not right.

O Lord, you will always know what is best for me.

O Lord, you will always know what I can't bear.

O Lord, you will always know all of my enemies.

O Lord, you will always warn me about danger.

O Lord, you will always let me choose to prolong my life or shorten my life.

O Lord, you will always love me and hate my sins.

O Lord, you will always love me and cleanse me from my sins.

O Lord, you will always love me and save me from my sins.

O Lord, you will always give me what is best for Your purpose for me.

O Lord, you will always love me, even if I don't love myself.

No One Can

No one can complete you like Jesus.

No one can encourage you like Jesus.

No one can help you like Jesus.

No one can comfort you like Jesus.

No one can lift you up like Jesus.

No one can give you joy like Jesus.

No one can understand you like Jesus.

No one can listen to you like Jesus.

No one can talk to you like Jesus.

No one can heal you like Jesus.

No one can cheer you up like Jesus.

No one can stand by you like Jesus.

No one can protect you like Jesus.

No one can give you strength like Jesus.

No one can be good to you like Jesus.

No one can be true to you like Jesus.

No one can make your dreams come true like Jesus.

No one can prosper you like Jesus.

No one can give you wisdom like Jesus.

No one can be real with you like Jesus.

No one can be there for you like Jesus.

No one can give you peace like Jesus.

No one can give you a favor like Jesus.

No one can give you good things like Jesus.

No one can change your life like Jesus.

No one can love you like Jesus.

No one can bless you like Jesus.

No one can sharpen your mind like Jesus.

No one can prolong your life like Jesus.

No one can educate you like Jesus.

No one can build you up like Jesus.

No one can help you to see the truth like Jesus.

No one can be trustworthy to you like Jesus.

No one can be faithful to you like Jesus.

No one can relieve you of your problems like Jesus.

No one can care for you like Jesus.

No one can be happy for you like Jesus.

No one can give you the right answers like Jesus.

No one can give you good advice like Jesus.

No one can be a friend to you like Jesus.

No one can give you what you need like Jesus.

Sometimes When We Believe

Sometimes when we believe that we are moving forward, we are not moving at all and are really standing still and going nowhere.

It can be frustrating when we put our best effort forward and get no good results.

Sometimes, when we believe that we have achieved something, we haven't made any improvement and it makes us feel so disappointing.

When it comes to doing something good in the name of the Lord, it can sometimes be hard to follow through because the devil will interfere with your efforts to achieve what you want to do in the name of our Lord and Savior Jesus Christ.

Sometimes when we believe that we have made it over our obstacles, there is another problem standing in our way and it's like a big pain in our neck that doesn't feel good.

Sometimes, when we believe that no one is affected by what we say and do, we can always read God's holy word to know that we have a good or bad effect on people because we can always believe God's holy word to be the truth over life achievements and disappointments.

You Can't Be Too

You can't be too wise and be wiser than God.

You can't be too smart and be smarter than God.

You can't be too genius and be more genius than God.

You can't be too brilliant and be more brilliant than God.

You can't be too free and more free than God.

You can't be too loving and be more loving than God.

You can't be too faithful and be more faithful than God.

You can't be too truthful and be more truthful than God.

You can't be too careful and be more careful than God.

You can't be too protective and be more protecting than God.

You can't be too trusting and be more trustworthy than God.

You can't be too humble and be more humble than God.

You can't be too patient and be more patient than God.

You can't be too giving and be more giving than God.

You can't be too strong and be stronger than God.

You can't be too undefeated and be more victorious than God.

You can't be too powerful and be more powerful than God.

You can't be too understanding and be more understanding than God.

You can't be too good and be more good than God.

You can't be too on time and be more on time than God.

You can't be too right and be more right than God.

You can't be too holy and be more holy than God.

You can't be too talkative and talk more than God.

You can't be too much of a listener and listen more than God.

You can't be too much of a judge and judge more than God.

You can't be too beautiful and be more beautiful than God.

You can't be too correct and be more correct than God.

You can't be too encouraging and be more encouraging than God.

You can't be too knowledgeable and be more knowledgeable than God.

You can't be too much of a doctor and be more of a healer than God.

You can't be too much of a lawyer and win more cases than God.

You can't be too much of an astronaut and be more out in the universe than God.

You can't be too much of a scientist and have more information about this world than God.

You can't be too much of an atheist for God to not reveal himself to you, especially if you are on your death bed.

Some Similarities

Human beings and animals have some similarities.

Human beings and animals have two eyes to see.

Human beings and animals have two ears to hear.

Human beings and animals have one nose to breathe out of.

Human beings and animals have one brain in their heads.

Human beings and animals have one mouth and one tongue.

God created human beings and animals with some similarities that you and I can see.

God created man and woman in His image but did not create the animals in His image.

Man and woman have a mind to think like God.

The animals can't think like that.

Men and women can choose from right and wrong.

The animals can't choose from right and wrong like we do.

Evolutionists believe that human beings evolved from apes, but apes are unthinking animals.

Why would God, in all His wisdom and perfection, stoop down out of His image to evolve a man and woman out of an ape or out of anything less than being in His image, which human beings can relate to but the animals can't?

Human beings and animals have some similarities.

Human beings and animals can procreate.

A man degrades himself if he believes that he evolved from an ape or anything other than what God created in His image.

Only human beings have some similarities with God.

The animals don't have those same similarities and cannot think and choose right from wrong.

Evolutionists can't degrade God's image, because anyone in their right mind would not want to believe that they evolved from an ape that God did not create in His image.

If People Try to Control You

If people try to control you with what they say, then what they say has flaws in it.

If people try to control you with what they believe, then what they believe has flaws in it.

People that have a lying tongue will try to control you and make you believe what they say.

If people try to control you with their ideas, then their theories have flaws in them.

If people try to control you on your job, then they are most miserable.

If people try to control you in your neighborhood, then they are nothing but trouble.

If people try to control you on the road, then they are reckless and want you to get in an accident.

If people try to control you in your house, then they are rotten to the bone.

If people try to control you in the church, then they are like leeches all over your body, sucking up all of your blood.

If people try to control you, then they are like the devil.

God didn't create us to control us.

God gave us free will, and that is a bad thing to controlling people.

I Had Lived in Darkness

I had lived in darkness and I believed that I was all right.

I believed that I was living a good life, but I lived in darkness.

I had rejected the light of the Lord shining all around me, and took the Lord's blessings with no true concern for what I was doing.

I had followed the ways of the world that enslaved me in the bondage of sin that I cherished.

I had lived in darkness that caused me to be a wanderer in life, because I had no real purpose.

That darkness had blinded my spiritual eyes so that I could not see that I was going to a dead end and would meet my fate in hell.

I had lived in darkness like a dog licking up his vomit that has no good taste to it.

The Lord didn't let me die in my darkness, even when I didn't deserve God's mercy and grace.

That darkness had deceived me and covered over my life like the sky filled with smoke.

I had lived in darkness and believed that my sinful life didn't have a bad effect on anyone else.

I just didn't care to search and find the Lord, who knew where I was in my darkness.

The Lord knew where I was in my darkness and he showed His pity on me and winked his eye at my ignorance.

That darkness tried to destroy me in my ignorance that looked all right in my eyes.

I had lived in darkness, but the Lord Jesus Christ didn't give up on me even though I was very numb to spiritual things and didn't care or want to know about them.

I am very glad today that I can feel the power of the Holy Spirit moving in my life so that I can love and obey Jesus Christ, who can shine through darkness and give His hope, love and truth to light up anyone's life.

Real, True Christians

Real, true Christians are the most giving people in this world.

Real, true Christians are the most trustworthy people in this world.

 Real, true Christians are the wisest people in this world.

Real, true Christians are the most peaceful people in this world.

Real, true Christians are the kindest people in this world.

Real, true Christians are the gentlest people in this world.

Real, true Christians are the sincerest people in this world.

Real, true Christians are the most real people in this world.

Real, true Christians are the most caring people in this world.

Real, true Christians are the most helpful people in this world.

Real, true Christians are the most forgiving people in this world.

Real, true Christians are the most respectful people in this world.

Real, true Christians are the most faithful people in this world.

Real, true Christians are the most joyful people in this world.

Real, true Christians are the most compassionate people in this world.

Real, true Christians are the most encouraging people in this world.

Real, true Christians are the most supportive people in this world.

Real, true Christians are the most truthful people in this world.

Real, true Christians are the healthiest people in this world.

Real, true Christians are the most vibrant people in this world.

Real, true Christians are the most selfless people in this world.

Real, true Christians are the most loving people in this world.

Real, true Christians are the most temperate people in this world.

Real, true Christians are the friendliest people in this world.

Real, true Christians are the most discerning people in this world.

Real, true Christians are the most fearless people in this world.

People who pretend to be Christians will sooner or later fail to meet the description of a real, true Christian, especially when trials come their way.

Real, true Christians are the most obedient people in this world as long as man's laws are in line with God's laws.

The Bible Is

The Bible is holy.

The Bible is correct.

The Bible is righteous.

The Bible is hope.

The Bible is faith.

The Bible is truth.

The Bible is inspiring.

The Bible is love.

The Bible is freedom.

The Bible is joyful.

The Bible is spiritual.

The Bible is encouraging.

The Bible is sacred.

The Bible is the past.

The Bible is the present.

The Bible is the future.

The Bible is always on time.

The Bible is trustworthy.

The Bible is goodness.

The Bible is peaceful.

The Bible is very sure.

The Bible is merciful.

The Bible is real.

The Bible is security.

The Bible is protection.

The Bible is wisdom.

The Bible is knowledge.

The Bible is education.

The Bible is humility.

The Bible is great.

The Bible is superb.

The Bible is fair.

The Bible is equality.

The Bible is justice.

The Bible is God speaking to us.

The Bible is prophecy.

The Bible is everything.

The Bible is temperance.

The Bible is deep.

The Bible is light in this dark world.

The Bible is a bridge over troubled waters.

The Bible is refreshing.

The Bible is gracious.

The Bible is victorious.

The Bible is a safe haven.

The Bible is strength.

The Bible is health.

The Bible is vigor.

The Bible is the word of God.

The Bible is the law of God.

The Bible is the same and will never change.

The Bible is authority.

The Bible is selfless.

The Bible is perfect.

The Bible is conviction.

The Bible is conversion.

The Bible is filled with the Holy Spirit.

The Bible is the GPS and road-map to heaven.

People Can go to Church

If people can go to work, people can go to church.

If people can go to school, people can go to church.

If people can go shopping, people can go to church.

If people can go to a funeral, people can go to church.

If people can go to a wedding, people can go to church.

If people can go fishing, people can go to church.

If people can go hunting, people can go to church.

If people can go to a football game, people can go to church.

If people can go to the amusement park, people can go to church.

If people can go on a cruise ship, people can go to church.

If people can travel, people can go to church.

If people can go mountain climbing, people can go to church.

If people can go camping, people can go to church.

If people can go hiking, people can go to church.

If people can go to a party, people can go to church.

If people can go on a picnic, people can go to church.

If people can go to a movie theater, people can go to church.

If people can go to the Oscars, people can go to church.

If people can go to concerts, people can go to church.

No one has an excuse to not go to church as long as they are in good health.

Going to church is a good start on your path to come to the Lord, and it gives you the opportunity to build a relationships with Him.

Going to church is a good start to change your life and live it unto the Lord.

Going to church is a good start that lets us know that we need to confess and repent of our sins and turn to God.

Going to church is a good start that lets us know that we didn't create ourselves because the Lord is our Creator and is worthy of our praise.

Is the Best Love

Loving You, my Lord, is the best love that I can always hold onto.

Loving You, my Lord, is the best love that I can always be very sure about.

Loving You, my lord, is the best love that I can always praise.

Loving You, my lord, is the best love that will always move my heart to glorify You.

Loving You, my lord, is the best love that will always keep me going strong.

Loving You, my lord, is the best love that I can always trust.

Loving You, my lord, is the best love that I can always depend on.

Loving You, my lord, is the best love that I can always believe to be right.

Loving You, my lord, is the best love that comforts my heart.

Loving You, my Lord and Savior Jesus Christ, is the best love that gives me a peace of mind and unspeakable joy.

If I don't love You, my Lord, then how can I truly love anyone else or myself, when loving You is the best love that I could ever give.

You loving me, O Lord, is the best love that I can ever receive in this life and the eternal life to come to me if I am saved in You, my Lord Jesus Christ.

O Lord, You are Always

O Lord, You are always good to me, even when I'm not good to You.

O Lord, You are always faithful to me, even when I'm not faithful to You.

O Lord, You always respect me, even when I don't respect You.

O Lord, You are always loyal to me, even when I am not loyal to You.

O Lord, You are always truthful to me, even when I'm not always truthful to You.

O Lord, You are always real with me, even when I'm not real with You.

O Lord, You are always with me, even when I'm not with You.

O Lord, You always treat me right, even when I don't treat You right.

O Lord, You always walk with me, even when I don't walk with You.

O Lord, You always talk to me, even when I don't talk to You.

O Lord Jesus Christ, you always love me, even when I don't love You.

O Lord, You always wait on me, even when I don't wait on You.

O Lord, You always listen to me, even when I don't listen to You.

O Lord, You are always a friend to me, even when I was not a friend to You.

Blow Our Minds

No one can blow our minds like the Lord Jesus Christ.

The Lord can blow our minds when He answers our prayers.

The Lord can blow our minds when we know that the Lord healed us from a sickness.

The Lord can blow our minds when we know that the Lord protected us from death.

No one can blow our minds like the Lord Jesus Christ.

The Lord can blow our minds when we know that the Lord gives us the strength to resist the devil's temptations.

The Lord can blow our minds when we know that the Lord worked things out for us.

The Lord can blow our minds when we know that the Lord opened our eyes to see the truth.

No one can blow our minds like the Lord Jesus Christ.

The Lord can blow our minds when we know without a doubt that the Lord brought us a long way to see this day.

The Lord can blow our minds when we know without a doubt that the Lord has renewed our lives for us to live unto Him day after day.

The Lord can blow our minds by giving us His Holy Spirit to teach us all truth in His holy word.

No one can blow our minds like the Lord Jesus Christ.

He is the only one to keep us in our right minds if our minds stay on Him in this world of so many corrupt minds.

The Lord Will Truly

The Lord will truly look out for us if we listen to and obey His voice speaking to us.

The Lord will truly cover our backs if we listen to and obey His voice speaking to us

The Lord will truly help us if we listen to and obey His voice speaking to us.

The Lord will truly encourage us if we listen to and obey His voice speaking to us.

The Lord will truly lift us up if we listen to and obey His voice speaking to us.

The Lord will truly encourage us if we listen to and obey His voice speaking to us.

The Lord will truly bless us if we listen to and obey His voice speaking to us.

The Lord Jesus Christ is always on time and speaks to us so clearly so that we have no excuse to not understand the voice of the Lord, who will truly tell us the truth that is in line with His holy word.

O Lord, You Will Not Fail Me

O Lord, You will not fail me even unto my death because You will give me eternal life when You come back again.

O Lord, You will not fail me when I get sick because You can heal me on Your time and You are always on time.

O Lord, You will not fail me through my hardships that are not too hard for You to move them out of my life.

O Lord, You will not fail me even if I fail myself in some kind of way because You are always victorious over sinners like me.

O Lord, You will not fail me on my bad days because You can use them to draw me closer to You.

O Lord, You will not fail me for as long as I live, even though that is short like one second to You who is eternal.

O Lord, You will never fail life because You are eternal life beyond my life that I can shorten and fail to see another day.

The Truth Will Set Me Free

O Lord, You brought me through hardships and is the truth that will set me free from lies.

O Lord, You brought me a long way and is the truth that will set me free from lies.

O Lord, You will supply all of my needs and be the truth that will set me free from lies.

O Lord, You never fail me and are always the truth that will set me free from lies.

O Lord, You won't let the devil tempt me with more than what I can bear and You will always be the truth that will set me free from lies.

O Lord, You answer my prayers and are always the truth that will set me free from lies.

O Lord, You give me life, health and strength and you are always the truth it will set me free from lies.

O Lord, You forgive me of my sins and You will always be the truth that will set me free from my lies.

O Lord, You want to save me for my sins and You are always the truth that will set me free from lies.

O Lord, You show mercy on me and are always the truth that will set me free from lies.

O Lord, You've given me a second chance and will always be the truth that will set me free from lies.

O Lord, You are patient with me and are always the truth that will set me free from lies.

O Lord, You give me strength and are always the truth that will set me free from lies.

O Lord, You brought me this far to see this day and You are always the truth that will set me free from lies.

O Lord, You are the truth to set me free from lying to myself and I will always tell my truth about what You brought me through.

O Lord, You love me and will be the truth that will set me free from the devil's lies.

O Lord, You never forsake me and are always the truth that will set me free from the devil's lies.

So Sure

Sometimes we can be so sure about doing something, but we didn't do it like we believed.

Sometimes we can be so sure about what we say, but our words will be so wrong.

Sometimes we can be so sure about where we are going, but we will get lost.

Sometimes we can be so sure about being right, but we will be so wrong.

Sometimes we can be so sure about knowing someone, when we don't know that person at all.

Sometimes we can be so sure about doing what we say, but we will change our minds.

Sometimes we can be so sure about what we believe, but we will doubt and not believe.

We can always be so sure about Jesus Christ loving us, even when we sin against Him.

We can always be so sure about Jesus never leaving or forsaking us just because we fall short of the glory of God.

We can always be so sure about Jesus Christ saving us from our sins, if we confess and repent of our sins and turn to Him.

On Our Christian Journey

On our Christian journey we will stumble sometimes.

On our Christian journey we will fall sometimes.

On our Christian journey we will make some mistakes.

On our Christian journey we will be misunderstood sometimes.

On our Christian journey we will be offended sometimes.

On our Christian journey we will offend others sometimes.

On our Christian journey will we will be criticized sometimes.

On our Christian journey we will be looked down on sometimes.

On our Christian journey we will be disrespected sometimes.

On our Christian journey we will be least favorable sometimes.

On our Christian journey we will be despised sometimes.

On our Christian journey we will be put down sometimes.

On our Christian journey we will be jealous sometimes.

On our Christian journey we will be envious of people sometimes.

On our Christian journey we will be talked bad about sometimes.

On our Christian journey we will be opinionated sometimes.

On our Christian journey we will disobey Jesus Christ sometimes.

On our Christian journey we will feel like giving up on Jesus sometimes.

On our Christian journey we will feel proud sometimes.

On our Christian journey we will feel self-sufficient sometimes.

On our Christian journey we will show favoritism sometimes.

On our Christian journey we will be selfish sometimes.

Our Christian journey is a journey of Jesus cleansing us of our sins.

Our Christian journey is a journey of Jesus saving us from our sins.

Our Christian journey is a lifetime journey of believing in Jesus Christ.

Our Christian journey is a journey of denying ourselves and picking up our crosses to follow Jesus Christ.

On our Christian journey we will be guilty of denying Jesus in our words and actions sometimes.

Our Christian journey is a lifetime journey of confessing and repenting of our sins.

There is Nothing More

There is nothing more real than the truth.

There is nothing clearer than the truth.

There's nothing more plain than the truth.

There is nothing more loving than the truth.

There is nothing more peaceful than the truth.

There is nothing friendlier than the truth.

There is nothing more believing than the truth.

There is nothing more convincing than the truth.

There is nothing more inspiring than the truth.

There is nothing braver than the truth.

There is nothing more reliable than the truth.

There is nothing more stable than the truth.

There is nothing more free than the truth.

There is nothing more powerful than the truth.

There is nothing more beautiful than the truth.

There is nothing more genius than the truth.

There is nothing more trustworthy than the truth.

There is nothing more joyful than the truth.

There is nothing more healing than the truth.

There is nothing more complete than the truth.

There is nothing greater than the truth.

There is nothing more fair than the truth.

There is nothing more right than the truth.

There is nothing more comfortable than the truth.

There is nothing more compassionate than the truth.

There is nothing more acceptable than the truth.

There is nothing wiser than the truth.

There is nothing more knowledgeable than the truth.

There is nothing more humble than the truth.

There is nothing more helpful than the truth.

There is nothing more alive than the truth.

There is nothing more spiritual than the truth.

There is nothing more healing than the truth.

There is nothing more satisfying than the truth.

There is nothing more superb than the truth.

There is nothing more superior than the truth.

Jesus Christ is the truth forever and ever beyond lies that will come to an end when Jesus Christ comes back again.

Just Downright Evil

There are many people who are not mentally ill; they are just downright evil.

Many people are just downright evil and love to kill people.

Many people are just downright evil and love to hurt people.

Many people are just downright evil and love to steal from people.

Many people are just downright evil and love to cheat people.

Many people are just downright evil and love to deceive people.

Many people are just downright evil and love to lie to people.

Many people are just downright evil and love to hate people.

There are many people who are mentally ill and are not evil.

There is more help for someone who is mentally ill than for someone who is just downright evil.

Psychiatric medicine can stabilize the mind of the mentally ill but that will not be effective for someone who is just downright evil.

The Lord hates evil, which is a lot worse than being mentally ill.

Everybody who is mentally ill is not a threat to society, but everybody who is just downright evil is a threat to society.

Will Increase More and More

Crimes will increase more and more before Jesus Christ comes back again.

Natural disasters will increase more and more before Jesus Christ comes back again.

Political strife will increase more and more before Jesus Christ comes back again.

Immorality will increase more and more before Jesus Christ comes back again.

Injustice will increase more and more before Jesus Christ comes back again.

Prejudices will increase more and more before Jesus Christ back again.

Atheism will increase more and more before Jesus Christ comes back again.

Spiritualism will increase more and more before Jesus Christ comes back again.

Evolution beliefs will increase more and more before Jesus Christ comes back again.

Rebellion will increase more and more before Jesus Christ comes back again.

Hate will increase more and more before Jesus Christ comes back again.

War will increase more and more before Jesus Christ comes back again.

Leaving the church will increase more and more before Jesus Christ comes back again.

Selfish ambition will increase more and more before Jesus Christ comes back again.

Homosexuality will increase more and more before Jesus Christ comes back again.

Same-sex marriages will increase more and more before Jesus Christ comes back again.

Pride will increase more and more before Jesus Christ comes back again.

Selfishness will increase more and more before Jesus Christ comes back again.

Deception will increase more and more before Jesus Christ comes back again.

Disobedient children will increase more and more before Jesus Christ comes back again.

Sexual assault will increase more and more before Jesus Christ comes back again.

Gossip will increase more and more before Jesus Christ comes back again.

Abuse will increase more and more before Jesus Christ comes back again.

Judging people will increase more and more before Jesus Christ comes back again.

Showing favoritism will increase more and more before Jesus Christ comes back again.

Craving attention will increase more and more before Jesus Christ comes back again.

Adultery will increase more and more before Jesus Christ comes back again.

Fornication will increase more and more before Jesus Christ comes back again.

Holding grudges will increase more and more before Jesus Christ comes back again.

Turning away from Jesus Christ will increase more and more before Jesus comes back again.

We Must

We must say what the Lord tells us to say because that will be the truth that the Lord will tell us to say in love.

The Lord will never tell us to say a lie, but the devil will tell us to lie.

We must do what the Lord tells us to do, regardless of how we feel.

We must do what the Lord tells us to do, regardless of how other people feel.

We must do what the Lord tells us to do, even if other people don't like it.

We must say what the Lord tells us to say, whether or not other people want to hear it.

We must say what the Lord tells us to say, whether people believe us or don't believe us.

The Lord will always tell us the right words to say to others.

The Lord will always tell us right things to do.

The Lord will never tell us to say anything wrong.

The Lord will never tell us to do anything wrong.

The Lord will always tell us to say what is in line with His holy word.

The Lord will always tell us to do what is in line with His holy word.

What the Lord tells us to say will be a blessing to someone.

What the Lord tells us to do will be a blessing to someone.

Everyone will not be blessed by what the Lord tells us to say or do, but we will be blessed by the Lord, who is always right in what He says and does.

All the Money in This World

All the money in this world can't heal your mental and emotional wounds.

All the money in this world can't heal your broken spirit.

You can sue someone for millions of dollars, but that can't get rid of your emotional pain.

All the money in this world can't erase your painful memories.

A lot of money can help ease your emotional pain, but Jesus Christ can heal your emotional and mental pain.

All the money in this world can't stop anyone from getting very sick with the flu.

All the money in this world can't stop anyone from getting sick with the coronavirus.

All the money in this world can't stop anyone from getting sick in the mind.

All the money in this world can't wipe away your tears.

All the money in this world can't heal your broken heart.

Having a lot of money can get you a lot of material things, but it can't keep your life from being torn apart.

All the money in this world can't do what Jesus Christ can do for you and me, because all the money in this world belongs to Jesus who owns the heavens and all the worlds.

Don't Put Anybody Down

Don't put anybody down, because you don't know what the Lord can do for someone.

You don't know how the Lord can bless someone's life.

Don't put anybody down because you don't know how the Lord can build someone up to achieve in life.

You don't know how high up the Lord can take someone.

You don't know where the Lord can take someone to.

Don't put anybody down, because you don't know how the Lord can change someone's life for the better.

Don't put anybody down, because the Lord can raise someone up above you and me.

You don't know what the Lord's plan is for someone.

Don't put anybody down, because the Lord can use anyone to help you and me.

Don't put anybody down, because everybody belongs to the Lord, who wants to save everybody.

You Can Believe

You can believe that you are strong, but you might be weak.

You can believe you're finished, but you might just be starting.

You can believe that you are right, but you might be wrong.

You can believe that you are good, but you might be bad.

You can believe that you are safe, but you might be in danger.

You can believe that you are fair, but you might be unfair.

You can believe that you are wise, but you might be foolish.

You can believe that you are intelligent, but you might be stupid.

You can believe that you are holy, but you might be a hypocrite.

You can believe that you are holding it together, but you might be falling apart.

You can believe that you are victorious, but you might be defeated.

You can believe that you are in control, but you might be out of control.

You can believe you have a relationship with the Lord, but you might be self-centered.

You can believe that you have favor with the Lord, but you might be holding onto some unconfessed sins.

You can believe that you are saved, but you might be lost.

You can believe that you are a Christian, but you might be showing favoritism to certain people.

As Long as You are Alive

As long as you are alive, you can choose to give your life to the Lord Jesus Christ.

Even if you are locked up in prison for the rest of your life, you can choose to confess and repent of your sins and live for Jesus in prison.

Jesus will bless your life, even in prison, where it's not a good place to live.

As long as you are alive, you can choose to live your life unto Jesus Christ, who will give you an abundance of life that the devil and his human agents can't rob you of, even if you are locked up in prison for life.

The Lord is patient with everyone and anyone who gives their life to Him before it's too late.

When you die, it's too late to confess and repent and live for Jesus.

The dead have no life to live anymore, so they cannot believe in Jesus Christ, but the righteous dead are saved.

As long as you are alive, you have a chance to choose who you will serve.

Serving the Lord is the best thing that you and I can do in our lives, regardless of the trials that we must go through for Jesus' name sake.

As long as you are alive, you can choose to come to the Lord, who is waiting on you with open arms of His everlasting love.

Having Greed for Worldly Gain

Having greed for worldly gain can cause anyone to steal.

Having greed for worldly gain can cause anyone to tell lies.

Having greed for worldly gain can cause anyone to kill.

Having greed for worldly gain can cause anyone to be discontent.

Having greed for worldly gain can cause anyone to be deceptive.

Having greed for world a gain can cause anyone to leave their spouse.

Having greed for worldly gain can cause anyone to leave their children.

Having greed for worldly gain can cause anyone to corrupt the church.

Having greed for worldly gain can cause anyone to leave the church.

Having greed for worldly gain can cause trouble in the home.

Having greed for worldly gain can cause anyone to turn their backs on the Lord Jesus Christ.

The Harder You Try

The harder you try, the more difficult it might be to get things done.

The harder you try, the more complicated it might be to achieve.

The harder you try, the more disappointing it might be to get things right.

The harder you try, the more frustrating it might be to finish what you started.

The harder you try, the more rugged it might be to smooth things out.

The harder you try, the more confusing it might be to clear things up.

The harder you try, the more expectations there might be to accomplish things.

The harder you try, the tougher it might be to change things.

The harder you try, the worse it might be to fix things.

You and I can try many things and they will never be as rewarding as giving Jesus Christ a try, which is something we will never regret.

Don't Think that You Can't

Don't think that you can't tell a lie, you better hold onto Jesus.

Don't think that you can't gossip, you better hold onto Jesus.

Don't think that you can't get angry, you better hold onto Jesus.

Don't think that you can't cheat, you better hold onto Jesus.

Don't think that you can't say something wrong, you better hold onto Jesus.

Don't think that you can't get in trouble, you better hold onto Jesus.

Don't think that you can't fall into sin, you better hold onto Jesus.

Don't think that you can't be judgmental, you better hold onto Jesus.

Don't think that you can't feel proud, you better hold onto Jesus.

Don't think that you can't make a mistake, you better hold onto Jesus.

Don't think that you can't be selfish, you better hold on to Jesus.

Don't think that you can't hold a grudge, you better hold onto Jesus.

Don't think that you can't do anything wrong, you better hold onto Jesus.

Don't think that you can't turn your back on Jesus, you better hold onto Jesus.

Strong Faith in the Lord

One way that we will know if we have strong faith in the Lord is to return tithes and offerings unto the Lord, even when we don't have much money left over.

Having strong faith in the Lord is to not worry about the trials that we go through and know that the Lord will not leave us or forsake us while we go through those trials.

Having strong faith in the Lord is to do what the Lord commands us to do, even if it takes us out of our comfort zone.

Having strong faith in the Lord is to not be afraid to call sin out by its rightful name, which is what the Lord wants us to do in love so that we do not push away a sinner who He wants to save from being lost in sin.

Shine Our Light

We are supposed to shine our light in this world where we Christians are to talk about Jesus and live unto Jesus in the presence of the people of the world.

We Christians are supposed to shine our light in our homes where we are to talk about Jesus and live unto Jesus in the presence of our family.

We are supposed to shine our light in the church where we Christians are to talk about Jesus and live unto Jesus in the presence of our church family.

We are supposed to shine our light with the gifts that the Lord gives to us to share with our family, church family and the people in our neighborhood where some of our neighbors will be blessed by our spiritual gifts from the Lord Jesus Christ.

Many Christians want to shine their light in the presence of the people of the world and don't really care about shining their light in the presence of their spiritual brothers and sisters in the church and in the presence of their own family.

We Christians Deal With

We Christians deal with truth, not with lies.

We Christians deal with reality, not fantasy.

We Christians deal with humility, not selfish pride.

When Christians deal with loving everyone, not showing favoritism.

We Christians deal with peace, not strife.

We Christians deal with hope, not doom.

We Christians deal with trials, not complacency.

We Christians deal with righteousness, not wickedness.

We Christians deal with moderation, not overindulgence.

We Christians deal with obedience unto the Lord, not rebellion unto the Lord.

We Christians deal with loving the Lord, not loving this world.

We Christians deal with being saved in Jesus Christ, not being lost in our sins.

We Christians deal with faith in the Lord Jesus Christ, not the things that we see in this world.

It Will Look Like
It was Evil From God

Back in the Bible days, it looked like it was evil from God when wicked nations were destroyed and men, women, boys and girls were killed.

It appeared to be an evil act of God that destroyed rebellious people back in the Bible days, but God did everything right.

How can it be evil in the righteousness of God, who is good all the time and knows how to work out the good that many people believed to be evil from God?

When God destroys whoever isn't like Him, it's for God's good cause, but the devil will used this to make God look evil.

Do we really believe that God would do anything evil to anyone, no matter how evil someone might be?

We know that evil is the opposite of good.

The Bible says that God is good, even when His wrath might look like it is evil.

It is a strange act for God to destroy what He created, but it's not an evil act for God to destroy what He created.

God is love and there is no evil in love.

It will look like it is evil from God when He destroys this world one day.

It will be a strange and righteous act from God to destroy all who rebel against Him, and His wrath will look evil to rebellious people who will meet their end on judgment day.

In Heaven

If we make it to heaven, we won't be sitting around doing nothing there.

We will be busy doing things in heaven.

Being busy for the Lord in this world is nothing compared to what we will be doing in heaven for the Lord.

What we are doing here on earth is just one drop of water in the bucket compared to an ocean of doing things in heaven.

We will never run out of things to do in heaven and the new earth that we will live on one day for being saved in Jesus Christ.

All the work on earth that we do in Jesus Christ's holy name is like a little pebble in the sand compared to the eternal work that will go on beyond the number of stars in one billion universes.

If we make it to heaven, our work for the Lord will never end so that other worlds will know that our love for Jesus is immeasurable beyond all existence that God created in his Son, Jesus.

A Self-Examination

A self-examination is to look at one's own flaws.

A self-examination is to look at one's own failures.

A self-examination is to look at one's own mistakes.

A self-examination is to look at one's own misfortunes.

A self-examination is to look at one's own imperfections.

A selfie examination is to look at one's own life.

A self-examination is to look at one's own faith in Jesus or not having faith in Jesus.

A self-examination is to look at oneself either loving Jesus or not loving Jesus.

A self-examination is to look at oneself either living for Jesus or not living for Jesus.

A self-examination is to look at oneself either giving the glory and praise to Jesus or not giving the glory and praise to Jesus.

A self-examination is to look at oneself either denying self and following Jesus or not denying self and following the devil.

The Fire of Trials

Every Christian will go through the fire of trials to be more and more like Jesus Christ.

Going through trials for Jesus' name sake will get rid of pride that is like throwing a bucket of cold water on every child of God.

Every Christian will go through the fire of trials to test their faith in Jesus Christ, who can quench the fire.

Fire burns hot, and no one wants to touch it or get burned, but every Christian will get burned by the devil for loving Jesus and keeping His Commandments that will heal our burns.

Every Christian will go through the fire of trials that Jesus went through without sin to save us from our sins.

The fire of trials will test our free will choice to choose to live for Jesus or to give into the devil's temptations while we go through our trials.

You Carry Me Through

O Lord, You carry me through the day because I have no strength on my own to get through the day without You.

O Lord, You carry me through my dreams in my sleep all night long.

O Lord, You wake me up in Your strength in the early morning so that I can thank You with praise unto You.

O Lord, You carry me through the things that I can't get through on my own intellect that can fail me.

O Lord, Your wisdom is the highest intellect to carry me through the foolishness in this world from day to day.

O Lord, my strength is broken like glass that I can step on and get badly cut and make me bleed.

Your strength, O Lord, will never break into pieces and will carry me through this broken world of sin that can't cut up Your mercy and grace.

O Lord, You carried me through all of my years with Your strength because Your love for me is forever and ever strong through my weaknesses that I can give to You, my Lord Jesus Christ, my Almighty strength.

Loves to Degrade Us Human Beings

The devil loves to degrade us human beings who God created in His image.

The devil loves to degrade us human beings and say we evolved from apes.

The devil loves to degrade us human beings and say we evolved from monkeys.

The devil loves to degrade us human beings and say we evolved from sea creatures.

The devil was not in on any of God's creations, especially not when He was creating a man and a woman.

The devil wants many people to believe that it was by chance that we exist, when we exist because of God.

The devil loves to degrade us human beings because he knows that we are not doomed to go to hell like he was doomed to go there with his fallen angels.

The devil loves to degrade God and say God is only an illusion to you and me, but the Bible and even nature lets you and me know that God is real.

Get High On

Many people will get high on voting on election day.

Many people will get high on trying to win the lottery.

Many people will get high on drugs.

Many people will get high on football Super Bowl games.

Many people will get high on gambling.

Many people will get high on the baseball World Series.

Many people will get high on the basketball world championship games.

Many people will get high on sex.

Many people will get high on concerts.

Many people will get high on family reunions.

Many people will get high on falling in love.

Many people will get high on getting a book published.

Many people will get high on food.

A Christian will get high on God's holy word.

A Christian will get high on prayer.

A Christian will get high on loving the Lord Jesus Christ and keeping His Commandments.

To be Like Jesus

We must treat everybody right to be like Jesus.

We must be fair to everybody to be like Jesus.

We must be kind to everybody to be like Jesus.

We must be honest with everybody to be like Jesus.

We must be good to everybody to be like Jesus.

We must be humble to everybody to be like Jesus.

We must be gentle with everybody to be like Jesus.

We must forgive everybody to be like Jesus.

We must respect everybody to be like Jesus.

We must be patient with everybody to be like Jesus.

We must be sincere to everybody to be like Jesus.

We must be real with everybody to be like Jesus.

We must love everybody to be like Jesus.

The Unseen

The unseen is all around us every day, and the angels are unseen.

The unseen is all around us every day, and God is unseen.

The unseen is more real than the seen.

All that we see we can take to be ordinary in this life, but all that is unseen to us we can take for granted like the unseen air that we breathe.

The unseen is ordinary to God every day that the unseen is more active than the seen.

The unseen is very busy around the clock when you and I, who see one another, need to get some sleep and be inactive.

You and I are limited to only seeing the seen, but our faith can be unlimited in the unseen God who gave us His only begotten Son who was seen by many people back in the Bible days.

Jesus Christ is unseen to us today, but we can believe in Him and be saved to get connected to the unseen spiritual world of God, who has the authority over the seen and unseen.

A Wolf in Sheep's Clothing

A wolf in sheep's clothing can pretend to be very friendly.

A wolf in sheep's clothing can pretend to be very kind.

A wolf in sheep's clothing can pretend to be very gentle.

A wolf in sheep's clothing can pretend to be very encouraging.

A wolf in sheep's clothing can pretend to be very supportive.

A wolf in sheep's clothing can pretend to be good.

A wolf in sheep's clothing can pretend to be humble.

A wolf in sheep's clothing can pretend be truthful.

A wolf in sheep's clothing can be very captivating.

A wolf in sheep's clothing can be very beautiful.

A wolf in sheep's clothing can be very convincing.

A wolf in sheep's clothing can speak eloquent words.

A wolf in sheep's clothing can disguise its true self.

A wolf in sheep's clothing can fool you and me.

A wolf in sheep's clothing can pretend to be so holy.

A wolf in sheep's clothing can pretend be so righteous.

A wolf in sheep's clothing can pretend to be a Christian.

A wolf in sheep's clothing can pretend to love you and me.

Only the Lord Jesus Christ knows every wolf in sheep's clothing.

Only Jesus Christ can always reveal a wolf in sheep's clothing to you and me.

Why Should We be Surprised?

Why should we be surprised if there is a mass shooting very close to where we live?

The Bible says that the devil is like a roaring lion, seeking whom he may devour.

Why should we be surprised if someone in our neighborhood area is shot and killed?

Why should we be surprised if someone in our neighborhood goes to jail?

The devil is running to and fro throughout the Earth to devour who he can devour.

So, why should we be surprised if a serial killer is very close to where we live?

Why should we be surprised if a child molester is very close to where we live?

Why should we be surprised if a rapist is very close to where we live?

Why should we be surprised if sex trafficking happens very close to where we live?

Why should we be surprised if drug trafficking happens very close to where we live?

The devil has his human agents, even in good neighborhood areas, who make crimes happen.

We children of God should not be surprised that this world will get worse in wickedness.

This world will get no better before Jesus Christ comes back again.

The Heart Can Have

The heart can have the hottest temperatures.

It can get very hot in the summertime when the temperatures can be over one hundred degrees.

Many people have gotten a heat stroke because they were out in the heat for too long.

The heart can have the hottest temperatures of anger that can be like an explosion of a nuclear bomb with temperatures over one thousand degrees.

The very hot temperatures of anger can bring on a heat stroke of violence and murder.

The heart can also have the coldest temperatures.

It can get very cold in the wintertime when temperatures get below zero degrees.

Many people have gotten frostbite and have frozen to death because they were out in the cold weather for too long.

The heart can have the coldest temperatures of prejudice that can bring on the frostbite of favoritism and can freeze dignity to death with hate.

The heart can be very sinful, but Jesus will not condemn the heart for its sins.

Instead, He will save the heart from its sins if the heart confesses and repent and believes in Jesus Christ to be saved.

God Can Use Animals

God can use animals to teach us to love.

God can use animals to teach us to be observant.

God can use animals to teach us to be patient.

God can use animals to teach us to forgive.

God can use animals to teach us to be humble.

God can use animals to teach us to be good.

God can use animals to teach us to be careful.

God can use animals to teach us to be obedient.

God can use animals to teach us to be thankful.

God can use animals to teach us to be joyful.

God can use animals to teach us to be in control of ourselves.

God can use animals to teach us to do right.

God can use animals to teach us to talk right.

God can use animals to teach us to not give up.

God created all the animals and God can surely use the animals to mend our brokenness.

Like an Unsolved Mystery

Some people will put their minds on doing something good and follow through with it, and some people will put their minds on something good and not follow through with it and be like an unsolved mystery.

We just don't always know why some people follow through and succeed, while some people don't follow through and are like an unsolved mystery.

Some people will try their best to treat everybody right and some people won't try their best to treat everybody right and will be like an unsolved mystery.

Only the Lord knows what everybody will do before an action is done, so to the Lord it's not an unsolved mystery.

There are people who don't know you and want the best for you, and there are some people who know you and don't want the best for you to be like an unsolved mystery.

There are people who will try their best to do what is right by what they know, and there are people who know what to do and don't do right to be like an unsolved mystery.

It's like an unsolved mystery that Lucifer in all of his beauty and perfection chose to rebel against God up in heaven, where he had everything except God's holy throne.

There are people who don't believe in Jesus Christ and will show some love to people, and there are people who profess to believe in Jesus Christ and will show respect of persons and be like an unsolved mystery.

The Devil is a Liar

The devil wants all white people to believe that all Black people are criminals.

The devil wants all Black people to believe that all white people are prejudiced.

The devil is a liar and he wants you and me to believe his lies.

Back in the slavery days there were some white people who help some Black people to escape from the south and live in the north.

Back in the Civil War, there were some Black soldiers who saved the lives of some white soldiers.

Today, some white people have some Black friends and some Black people have some white friends.

Today, some white people are married to Black people.

The devil is a liar and he wants you and me to believe his lies.

If all white people were prejudiced, there would not be any white and Black people living in the same neighborhood today.

If all Black people were criminals, there would not be any prosperous Black people.

God is too good to allow all white people to be prejudiced.

God is too good to allow all Black people to be criminals.

The devil hates that God is good to white people and Black people, so we should not be ignorant of the truth that is always victorious over the devil's lies.

The devil wants all white people to believe that all Black people are lazy and don't want to work.

Some Black people are hard-working people and don't get paid the money they deserve to get.

The devil wants all Black people to believe that all white people can't be trusted and are deceiving.

There are some trustworthy white people who will do what they say.

The devil is a liar and he wants you and me to believe his lies, no matter if we are white or black or any other race of people.

If You Feel Depressed

If you feel depressed about something, have a heart-to-heart talk with Jesus, who knows exactly how you feel.

You can always talk to Jesus about what is heavy on your mind, because Jesus will comfort you after you have opened up to Him.

You will feel so much better when you talk to Jesus and ask Him to help you and give you strength to keep going on when you feel like giving up.

The devil loves to cause you and me to feel depressed and get our minds off the Lord Jesus Christ, who you and I can think on and have peace of mind.

Anyone can feel depressed, especially if they have lost a loved one who was very close.

Even Jesus felt depressed when the heavy weight of the sins of the whole world were upon Him.

Jesus prayed to His Heavenly Father asking if it was possible that the hour might pass for Him.

And he said, "Abba, Father, all things are possible unto Thee. Take away this cup from me, nevertheless, not what I will, but Thou wilt."

Jesus was depressed to say those words to His heavenly Father who strengthened Jesus in the garden of Gethsemane.

If you get depressed about something that is going on in your life, pray to Jesus and talk to Him — it doesn't always have to be a long conversation.

You can make your prayers short and from your heart to Jesus, who can keep your depression away from you if you pray to Him every day.

Jesus can keep you strong in your mind, but the devil loves to make you and me weak in our minds so we feel depressed.

There is nothing that Jesus can't do for you and me, who can always talk to Jesus even if we feel depressed.

Depression is not too hard for Jesus to get rid of.

If you and I truly believe that Jesus Christ is the best psychiatrist, the best psychologist and the best therapist, then we are on our way to being made spiritually hole in our minds.

The devil will try to make us feel depressed, but if we talk to Jesus and pour out our hearts out to Him, we will feel so much better.

If we don't feel so much better, then we just don't believe that Jesus is all-powerful above depression.

All good things are from the Lord Jesus Christ.

It's a good thing to see a psychiatrist, psychologist and therapist because the Lord Jesus Christ uses many of them to heal people from their depression.

Many people have strong faith in the Lord that works for them regardless of feeling depressed.

They believe that prayer alone will get rid of depression, and there's nothing wrong with that.

Prayer alone does work for many people and helps them to get over their depression without needing a psychiatrist, psychologist or therapist to help them.

Our Free Will

Our free will is between Jesus and the devil.

Our free will is between good and evil.

Our free will is between right and wrong.

Our free will is between our thoughts and words.

Our free will is between our thoughts and actions.

With our free will choice, we can choose to live unto the Lord God Jesus Christ or choose to live for the devil.

With our free will choice, we can choose to do good or do evil.

With our free will choice, we can choose to do right or do wrong.

With our free will choice, we can choose to think before we talk.

With our free will choice, we can choose to think before we act.

With our free will choice, we can choose to speak before we act.

With our free will choice, we can choose to keep our eyes on Jesus or keep our eyes on this world.

Between our ideas and reasoning is our free will.

Between our opinions and reasoning is our free will.

Between our opinions and educated guesses is our free will.

Between our poverty and prosperity is our free will.

Between our bondage and freedom is our free will.

Between life and death is our free will.

Our free will is the median between our purpose in life and our perseverance in life.

Our free will is the median between our blessings and misfortunes.

Our free will is God's masterpiece work that the angels gaze at with admirable words to say.

The devil hates our free will, because he can't control us no matter how much he tempts us who can choose to believe in Jesus Christ and be saved.

Struggles

Many people believe that they can get through their own struggles in life.

Many people don't believe that the Lord will help them to get through their struggles.

Many people believe that they can rely on their own strength to overcome their struggles.

Many people don't believe that they need strength from the Lord to overcome their struggles.

Believing that you can get through your struggles without the help of the Lord is like being blind and wanting to drive a car.

Believing that you can get through your struggles without the help of the Lord is like jumping out of a plane without a parachute.

Believing that you can get through your struggles without the help of the Lord is like drinking poison so you get sick and die.

Going through struggles and believing that you don't need the Lord to help you through your struggles is like jumping into hot flames of fire where you will surely burn up.

Many people believe that they don't need the Lord to help them get through their struggles but those struggles will sooner or later get the best of them if they don't trust the Lord to help them overcome those struggles.

Because of being born in sin, we all go through some struggles in life and will surely need the Lord to help us through them.

If you believe that you can get through your struggles without the help of the Lord Jesus Christ, it is like seeing a poisonous snake crawling toward you, then stooping down to pick it up as if it won't bite you.

If you believe that you can get through your struggles on your own strength, it's like turning your nose up at the Lord and telling Him that His strength can't do anything to help you overcome your struggles.

A Changing Church

A changing church is not the church of Jesus Christ, He will never change His holy law.

We live in a changing world where the church of Jesus Christ will remain the same with real, true Christians being different from the people of the world.

A changing church will give in to false doctrines but the church of Jesus Christ stands firm on the truth of God's holy word.

A changing church will change with the people of the world to be a friend to the world to please the world.

The church of Jesus Christ will remain the same so that it can spread the gospel of Jesus Christ to all the world.

The church of Jesus Christ is a friend to Jesus and works to please Jesus in winning souls to Him.

A changing church will try to change God's word into false teachings of theories and opinion and self-exaltations to put Jesus on the back bench of the church.

A changing church is like a tornado destroying everything in its path.

A changing church is blown away by the winds of lies, but the church of Jesus Christ is built on the rock of Jesus who is the truth that will never change.

A changing church is the devil's pot of stew that even many professed Christians will eat and vomit out and lick it back up like a dog.

The church of Jesus Christ is filled with the fruit of the Holy Spirit for every true child of God to eat spiritual things and never get spiritually nauseated or vomited.

The head of a changing church is this changing world that can't change God, who is true to His holy word even though many church folks will try to change the words into their own way of living far from the truth of God.

Our Actions will Talk a lot More

Our actions will talk a lot more than the words that we say.

We can shut our mouths and be silent, but our actions are not silent and talk a lot through our body language.

Our actions will talk to people when we run out of words to say.

Our actions will talk all the time and will very often tell the truth about me and you.

We don't usually pretend with our actions, because they are very often real and tell the truth a lot more than our words.

Many actors will pretend with their actions as they portray things to be real, and feeble-minded people may have a hard time telling the difference between what is real and what is pretend.

Our actions don't run out of words to say, whether they are good actions or bad actions that will very often tell the truth even with our mouth is shut.

Jesus' actions talked a lot more than His divine words, because all of Jesus' actions were perfect with no pretending.

Jesus was always real with no playacting involved when He lived here in this world where our actions will talk a lot more than what we say out of our mouths.

Actors love to live a normal life with real true actions, but they are with their family and friends who they will not pretend with in their words and actions.

The actions of every Christian are closely watched, a lot more than the actions of the people of the world who can also go to church and profess to be a Christian with pretend actions that can look holy and righteous while holding office positions in the church.

Our actions will talk a lot more than what we say out of our mouths.

When real, true Christians have real, true good actions, a lot more than words about Jesus Christ.

When Jesus lived here on earth without sin, He had no pretend words and no pretend actions.

Jesus' perfect actions talked a lot more than His perfect words.

Actors are very good at making their actions look real, but they are not real.

Whether our actions are real or pretend, our actions will talk a lot more than what we say out of our mouths.

We Must Solely Depend

We must solely depend on God's intelligence.

Our intelligence will fail us.

We must solely depend on God's wisdom.

Our wisdom will fail us.

We must solely depend on God's mind.

Our minds will fail us.

We must solely depend on God's ways.

Our ways will fail us.

We must solely depend on God's heart.

Our hearts will fail us.

We must solely depend on God's will.

Our will fails us every time.

We must solely depend on God Almighty hand.

Our hands will fail us.

We must solely depend on God's all-seeing eyes.

Our eyes will fail us.

We must solely depend on God's holy Word.

Our words will fail us.

We must solely depend on God's reasons.

Our reasons will fail us.

We must solely depend on God's everlasting love.

Our love will fail us.

We must solely depend on God's everlasting life.

Our lives will fail us.

We must solely depend on God the father, God the Son and God the Holy Spirit.

Our sinful nature will surely fail us.

We must solely depend on God's son, Jesus Christ, to save us from our sins.

Our works will fail to save us from our sins.

We must solely depend on God's son, Jesus Christ, to take us to heaven when He comes back again.

We don't have our own power over death to raise ourselves from the dead and go to heaven before Jesus Christ comes back again.

Perfect But Not Perfect to Have Sins to Confess

Job was a perfect and upright man in the eyes of God, but Job was not perfect to have sins to confess and repent to God.

Job was perfect for not wanting to sin against God.

Job was perfect for not willing to sin against God.

When God cleanses us from living in our sins, we are made perfect to not want to commit those sins against God again.

If God cleanses you from smoking cigarettes, you are perfect to not want to smoke anymore cigarettes.

If God cleanses you from telling lies, you are perfect to not want to tell any more lies.

If God cleanses you from fornicating, you are perfect to not want to fornicate anymore.

We are not perfect to have sins, but we can be perfect from the sins that the Lord God cleansed us from.

If we confess and repent of our sins that we are living in, the Lord God Jesus Christ will forgive us and cleanse us from those sins so that we can be perfect to not want to commit those sins against Him anymore.

We have sins that we are not aware of to not be perfect to have unseen sins.

Just because Job was a perfect and upright man in the eyes of God does not mean that Job had no sins to confess and repent to God.

Some people will say that practice makes perfect, and we can reach to some perfections in our life, especially for confessing and repenting of our sins to the Lord.

Those sins that Jesus Christ forgives us and cleanses us of are those sins that are gone for us to be perfect and not wanting to have a desire to commit those sins again.

Black is Right for Me

Black is right for me to love the color of my skin, even if everyone else hates the color of my skin.

Black is right for me to believe that I am somebody who can make this world a better place to live in, regardless of being stereotyped.

Black is right for me to hope for a better tomorrow in my life, no matter what I go through today.

Black is right for me to accept who I am being a Christian black man, regardless of the prejudices that surround me day after day.

Black is right for me to enjoy holding onto and never letting go of my Black fulfillment.

Black is right for me to cherish that I am Black with a heart to respect everybody.

Black is right for me to learn from my mistakes and live a life of doing what is right.

Black is right for me to not judge anybody who God will judge.

Black is right for me to tell the truth from my heart to all the world.

Black is right for me to not want to change from being Black because God colored the night black in the black universe with His crayons.

Black is right for me to not bleach my skin to look different from what God has given me.

Black is right for me to be proud of every day, regardless of racism.

Black is right for me to get a good night's sleep and wake up well rested to start a new day being Black.

Black is right for me to believe in Jesus Christ, who shows no respect of persons and loves me and wants to save my soul.

Black is right for me to have no excuse not to give God my best efforts in this life.

Black is right for me to give this world my testimonies about what the Lord brought me through in my life.

Black is right for me to humble myself before the Lord, who doesn't care whether I am Black, white, brown, red or yellow to confess my sins and repent of my sins onto Him.

Black is right for me to give God all the glory and praise that He deserves beyond my blackness.

Black is right for me to carry on my Black ancestor's dreams to make sure they do not fade away in this world of uncertain days.

Black is right for me to never give up on my Lord and Savior Jesus Christ, who created me to be Black and who no one can degrace and get God's approval.

Black is right for me to go to heaven when Jesus Christ comes back again on the clouds of glory for the angels to take me up in and see no color barriers.

Black is right for me to be a blessing to all of my spiritual brothers and sisters, no matter what the color of their skin.

Black is right for me to have no age limit to make achievements in my life.

Black is right for me to choose to make good choices in my life.

Black is right for me to use my common sense that God gave to me.

Black is right for me to know my limits and not overdo things.

Black is right for me to trust my blackness and treat everybody right.

Black is right for me to be in control of myself, even if trouble comes my way.

Black is right for me to not hide my blackness from this world that I don't owe my life to because I owe my life to God.

Black is right for me to never deny that I am Black and not cheat my way through life.

Black is right for me to live my life unto the Lord Jesus Christ, who will never discriminate when giving His love, mercy and grace to me.

Black is right for me to love even my enemies, who can kill my body but not my spirit.

Black is right for me to pray to the Lord with my broken prayers that the Holy Spirit has to fix and make right before God.

Black is right for me to love my neighbors and to love myself for being Black.

Black is right for me to reach up high in life that I will bring myself down from if I know to do right by the Lord and don't do it.

Black is right for me, even if Black is not right for anyone else, as if I am the only one who is Black.

Black is right for me to believe that the color of my skin is the right complexion for me to own it every day.

Black is right for me to lay down and close my eyes into the black, dark unconsciousness that I trust to not harm me in my deep sleep.

Black is right for me to dream away in the black dark and wake up in the consciousness of my blackness.

Black is right for me to honor its presence upon my body that I can joyfully live in every day that my blackness is right for me to live in this world of colorful people of every race.

God created the color of white, the color of black, the color of brown and the color of red and the color of yellow to paint this world and beautify His creation of the human race.

Many People will Believe that Luck

Many people will believe that luck is more powerful than God.

Many people will believe that luck spare their lives from death.

They don't believe that God spared their lives from death.

Many people will give luck the glory and praise above God, who deserves all the glory and praise.

Many people will believe that luck will bless them, but blessings are from the Lord God Jesus Christ.

Many people will believe that luck is more powerful than God, who all good things come from.

Many people will believe that good things come from luck, but that is like a balloon that will burst if you stick a sharp pin in it.

Luck is a household word in many people's homes where God is not spoken from sunup to sundown.

Many people will live for luck to make good things happen to them, when it's truly the Lord God Jesus Christ who makes good things happen to us all who don't deserve anything good from the Lord.

Luck is only a feel-good word to say, but God is more real than anyone we see and more real than anything we can't see because nothing can rise above God.

Luck will never rise above God, who created even the unseen that luck can't touch with it's unrealistic spoken words.

There are People

There are people who will complain about anything and will feel good about it.

There are people who have no cares about anyone but themselves.

There are people who love to be the center of attention and might do something bad to get the attention they want.

There are people who will put their lives in danger and joke about it like it's no big deal to them.

There are people who believe that they are always right about what they say, even when they are wrong and they don't want to see it.

There are people who will tell lies and believe that it's the truth, even if no one believes them.

There are people who will act like they are rich and have plenty of money to spend, but they're really as poor as a stray dog or cat.

There are people who don't believe in love, but when love approaches them and speaks to them they will respond to love without any hesitation.

There are people who stray away from Jesus Christ and will use His holy name like it's just an ordinary word.

There are people who will go to church and doubt what Jesus can do for them in their trials that they allow to cause them to have ill feelings about their faith in Jesus.

There are people who don't believe that there is a God, but they want to be a god in this fallen world where death will take them to the grave, while God is the origin of life to live forever and ever.

There are people who don't see a need to change for the better, but they see a need to want to change the Bible scriptures to fit in with their unchanging, rebellious lifestyle.

The Name of Every Human Being

The Lord knows the name of every star being more than all the pebbles on the beach sands all around the world.

The Lord knows the name of every human being who ever lived and is alive today.

All the information in the computers all around this world is no match for the Lord God, who knows all things in heaven and earth and in all other worlds.

The Lord knows the names of every creature in all the other worlds that didn't fall into sin when sin in this world has tarnished the names of all the dead and all the living.

The Lord knows the names of every human being dead and alive.

The Lord will give a new name to every human being who will enter into heaven when Jesus Christ comes back again.

Only the Lord knows the names of every human being who ever lived and is alive today.

Only the Lord can speak everybody's name at the same time without leaving out one name.

The Lord God knows the names of all the stars being more in number than all the pebbles in the beach sand all around the world.

It's not complicated to the Lord to know the names of all the angels in heaven and all the fallen angels too.

Can you and I ever imagine knowing the names of all of the angels in heaven, all of the names of everyone who makes it to heaven and all the names of all the creatures in all the other worlds?

If we make it to heaven, we will get to know every existing name of all of God's creations and we just don't know how long it will take us to know everybody's name in heaven and in other worlds.

We will live forever and ever and have plenty of time to get to know everybody's names.

We will have a perfect memory and get to know everybody's names that the Lord God knows with His infallible memory.

The Front Door and Back Door

When we were born into this world, we came through the front door of this world that has many rooms made of choices that we will make in our lives.

The front door of this world is always open for newborn babies, but we will one day leave out the back door of this world to go to the grave.

The front door of this world is open for you and me to walk through and enter into the house of this world that has many rooms of days and nights that we can pray unto the Lord without ceasing.

When we were born into this world, we came through the front door of this world that God keeps open for His grace to also walk through with us.

God's grace gives us all a chance to choose the right room that will have the spiritual things of God for you and me to believe in Jesus Christ and be saved before we leave out the back door of this world and go to the grave.

In the beginning of God's creation, this world only had a front door for Adam and Eve to walk through and enter into a perfect world with no back door to leave out of and go to the grave.

Because of Adam sinning against God, Adam created the back door of this world for all of us to leave out of and go to the grave one day.

That will happen if Jesus Christ doesn't come back again during our lifetime in this world.

When we were born into this world, we came through the front door of this world and entered into many rooms in the house of this world where the Lord is waiting on everybody to choose to enter into His room of confession and repentance onto Him and live onto him before leaving out the back door of this world.

As we live, we walk through the front door of this world that has many rooms of distractions in the house of this world, but we will one day leave out the back door of this world and hopefully join the righteous dead who Jesus will raise and take through the front door of heaven having no back door.

This Whole World is a Prison

This whole world is a prison and only Jesus has the keys to unlock the cell doors.

We all are prisoners of sin that we were born in, and only Jesus can drop all of our misdemeanors and felony charges of sin through His precious blood that was shed on the cross for you and me.

This whole world is a prison, where so many people are locked up in the chains of their sins for not confessing and repenting of their sins unto the Lord Jesus Christ, who has the keys to unlock the chains and set us free from living in sin.

We all are locked up in this world because of our sinful nature that keeps us from traveling to other worlds that are free from sin.

Jesus won't allow us to travel to other worlds because our sins would cause other worlds to keep us out of their perfect worlds.

We are a prisoner of sin if we don't believe in Jesus Christ, who will save us from our sins if we confess and repent and live our lives unto Him.

Because of our sinful nature, we have no freedom to travel back-and-forth to heaven and to other worlds like the angels in heaven who have no sin.

We all are stuck here on earth until Jesus Christ comes back again to take us out of this prison world if we are saved in Him.

What looks like freedom to us in this sinful world is imprisonment to the angels in heaven and to those in other worlds who have no sins.

We all are stuck here on earth until Jesus Christ comes back again to take us out of this prison world if we are saved in Him.

What looks like freedom to us in the sinful world is imprisonment to the angels in heaven and to other worlds that are forever and ever free in heaven and throughout the infinite universes.

Only Jesus has the keys to unlock the cell doors of this world and set us free from our sinful charges, if we choose to love Him and keep His Commandments.

Jesus is eternal freedom beyond the angels and other worlds that are forever free in Jesus, while we live in this prison world where the devil is the chief prison officer who loves to lock us up in our sins.

Astronauts have traveled to the moon, but never to heaven and other worlds where living creatures are perfect without sin beyond this whole world that is a prison.

Jesus once lived in this prison world, and the devil tried to lock Jesus up here, but he failed. Jesus rose from the grave with victory and unlocked the cells of this world to set all men, women, boys and girls free from the charges of sin.

Knows Its Duty

The sun knows its duty to shine all day long.

The moon knows its duty to glow all night long.

The stars know their duty to sparkle all night long.

The ground knows its duty to hold together every day and every night.

The grass knows its duty to cover the ground.

The trees know their duty to stay rooted in the ground.

The house knows its duty to shelter you and me.

The vehicle knows its duty to take you and me on the road.

The wind knows its duty to blow in different directions.

The air knows its duty to let us breathe in and out of our noses.

The sky knows its duty to open wide high up over us.

A mountain knows its duty to stay solid up to its highest peak.

An airplane knows its duty to carry passengers across the sky.

A river knows its duty to flow into the ocean.

The oceans know their duty to cover three-fourths of the land.

The seasons know their duty to change every three months.

The dark clouds know their duty to empty the rain out of the clouds.

Money knows its duty to buy and sell and save.

Material things know their duty to be temporary.

This world knows its duty to one day pass away.

Many people don't know that it's their duty to love God and keep His Commandments — that is the whole duty of man.

Many church folks know that it's their duty to love God and keep His Commandments, but they believe that they are saved through God's grace and don't have to keep the Commandments.

Many people don't know that it's their duty to work out their own soul's salvation.

They depend on their pastors to work out their soul's salvation, but the pastor can't represent them before God who will we will all face up to for ourselves in God's judgment.

Time knows its duty to give you and me borrowed time to make our election sure in Jesus Christ before our time runs out in the land of the living.

Jesus is Closer to Us

Jesus is closer to us than our reflection in the mirror showing us its close connection with us.

Jesus is closer to us than our shadow showing us its close connection with us so it moves when we move our bodies.

Jesus is closer to us than the skin on our bodies showing us its close connection with us when we feel it all over our bones.

Jesus is closer to us than our minds showing us its close connection with us when we think.

Jesus is closer to us than our hearts showing us its close connection with us who have motives and intentions.

Jesus is closer to us than our lives showing us its close connection with us as we live.

Jesus is closer to us than our destiny showing us its close connection with us when we make choices.

Jesus is closer to us than death that can show us i's close connection with us when we die.

Jesus Christ, our Lord and Savior, created us to love and obey Him to show us our closer connection with Him every day and in the eternal life that He will give to us beyond our earthly days if we are saved in Him.

Jesus is closer to us than all that we say and do showing us His close connection with us for as long as we live.

Jesus is closer to us than our dreams that show us their close connection with us when we lay down to sleep.

Jesus is closer to us than anyone and anything in this world and up in heaven because Jesus is our creator God who wonderfully made us to choose or not to choose to connect with him more than connecting with whatever is below him.

Jesus is closer to us than all seen and unseen things showing us their close connection with us in surrounding us with their presence all around us.

Nothing can separate us from the strong connecting love of Jesus, no matter if we connect ourselves more to the creatures than to Jesus our Creator God.

Jesus is closer to us than our existence showing us its close connection with us because of Jesus who gave up His life on the cross and rose from the grave for you and me to exist today and get closer and closer to Him before it's too late.

For Jesus To

No teardrop is too grievous for Jesus to dry it up.

No heartache is too broken for Jesus to heal.

No trouble is too bad for Jesus to get rid of.

No problem is too hard for Jesus to work out.

No one is too lost in sin for Jesus to save.

No one is too proud for Jesus to humble.

No one is too weak for Jesus to strengthen.

No one is too sick for Jesus to make well.

No one is too sad for Jesus to give joy to.

No one is too poor for Jesus to prosper.

No one is too bad for Jesus to forgive.

No one is too good for Jesus to see no bad in him or her.

No one is too right for Jesus to see no wrong in him or her.

No one is too small for Jesus to make great.

No one is too ignorant for Jesus to give knowledge to.

No one is too knowledgeable for Jesus to teach.

No one is too faithful for Jesus to test.

No one is too wicked for Jesus to change.

No one is too foolish for Jesus to make wise.

No one is to holy and to righteous for Jesus to see no sin in him or her.

No one is too confusing for Jesus to understand.

No one can be too dead for Jesus to raise from the grave when he comes back again.

No one is too alone for Jesus to talk to you.

No one is too real for Jesus to see no pretense.

No one is too educated for Jesus to expand his or her mind.

No one is too unhealthy for Jesus to make healthy.

No one is too feeble-minded for Jesus to come into his or her mind and give it assurance in Him.

All the Time Until Eternity

I want to love You, O Lord, all the time until eternity.

I want to obey You, O Lord, all the time until eternity.

I want to have hope in You, O Lord all the time until eternity.

I want to follow You, O Lord, all the time until eternity.

I want to trust You, O Lord, all the time until eternity.

I want to believe in You, O Lord, all the time until eternity.

I want to praise You, O Lord, all the time until eternity.

I want to glorified You, O Lord, all the time until eternity.

I want to hold onto You, O Lord, all the time until eternity.

I want to keep my eyes on You, O Lord, all the time until eternity.

I want to depend on You, O Lord, all the time until eternity.

I want to have faith in You, O Lord, all the time until eternity.

I want to keep my mind on You, O Lord, all the time until eternity.

I want to give my heart to You, O Lord, all the time until eternity.

I want to give my soul to You, O Lord, all the time until eternity.

I want to be a witness of You, O Lord, all the time until eternity.

I want to talk to You, O Lord, all the time until eternity.

I want to be with You, O Lord, all the time until eternity.

I want to listen to You, O Lord, all the time until eternity.

I want to walk with You, O Lord, all the time until eternity.

I want to uplift Your holy name, O Lord, all the time until eternity.

I want to give testimonies about You, O Lord, all the time until eternity.

I want to think on You, O Lord, all the time till eternity.

I want to work for You, O Lord, all the time until eternity.

I want to live my life unto You, O Lord, all the time until eternity.

I want to be joyful in You, O Lord, all the time until eternity.

I want to have peace in You, O Lord, all the time until eternity.

I want to be humble unto You, O Lord, all the time until eternity.

I want to give You my talent, O Lord, all the time until eternity.

I want to give You my tithes and offerings, O Lord, all the time until eternity.

I want to give You my time, O Lord, all the time until eternity.

I want to give You my will, O Lord, all the time until eternity.

I want to give You my best, O Lord, all the time until eternity.

I want to be saved in You, O Lord all the time until eternity.

I need You, O Lord, all the time until eternity that is You, my Lord Jesus Christ.

Loves to Hide the Truth

One day in the morning, I went to the Walmart store to buy some vegan butter.

When I walked up to the freezer where the vegan butter is supposed to be kept, I didn't see the vegan butter there.

The freezer was filled with different kinds of butter on the shelves.

At the exact location where I usually see the vegan butter, the shelf was filled with I Can't Believe It's Not Butter.

I just stood there trying to see where the vegan butter was.

Then the Lord spoke to me and said, "Look behind the butter that is stacked up on the shelf."

I listened to the Lord and looked behind the butter labeled I Can't Believe It's Not Butter.

Then I saw the vegan butter and some more vegan butter hiding behind the I Can't Believe It's Not Butter.

Just by experiencing that situation, the Lord showed me that the devil loves to hide the truth behind his lies every day.

The devil doesn't want you and me to know the truth, especially the truth of God's holy word.

If I didn't listen to the Lord and look behind the containers that said I Can't Believe It's Not Butter, then I would never have seen the vegan butter.

If you and I look behind the devil's lies, we will see the truth that the Lord will show to us no matter what truth it may be.

The truth is like the vegan butter that is much better to eat for our health.

The devil loves to hide the truth behind his lies, but the Lord will speak to us who can choose or not choose to listen to Him telling us to look behind the devil's lies to see the truth that will set us free from lies.

Some Bad Beliefs About God

It's not easy to talk to someone who has some bad beliefs about God.

There are people who believe that God is mean.

There are people who believe that God is hard on them.

There are people who believe that God can't help them.

There are people who believe that God is unfair.

There are people who believe that God doesn't love them.

There are people who believe that God can't do anything for them.

There are people who have some bad beliefs about God.

There are people who believe that God doesn't care about them.

There are people who believe that God doesn't exist.

There are people who believe that God is weak.

There are people who believe that God didn't have anything to do with them being successful.

It's not easy to be around someone who has some bad beliefs about God.

There are people who believe that God doesn't see them.

There are people who believe that God doesn't hear them.

There are people who believe that God doesn't have a heart.

There are people who believe that God will let them get away with their evil deeds.

There are people who believe that God is a liar.

There are people who believe that God is not good.

There are people who believe that God fails them.

There are people who believe that God is a waste of their time.

There are people who believe that they can con God.

There are people who believe that they can deceive God.

There are people who believe that they can outsmart God.

There are people who believe that they can charm God.

There are people who have some bad beliefs about God, but God will never change from loving everyone regardless of their bad beliefs about Him.

There are people who have some bad beliefs about God, but they will never change His holy word about sending His only begotten Son to this world to save us from our sins, regardless of bad beliefs that will never overrule God.

Some People Will

Some people will act like you and I are wrong for wanting to back out of the parking lot and will block you and me from backing out.

Some people will look at you and me like we are wrong for standing behind them in the grocery store checkout line.

Some people will walk by you and me and avoid eye contact with you and me as if we are not there for them to see us.

Some criticizing people will watch you and me to see if we will say or do something wrong so that they can be right about the bad things that they say about you and me.

Some people will not want you and me to talk about how we feel, because they seem to think that's a problem for them and will pretend that they are made of steel and can't be broken down.

Some people will want to get in your business and my business and gossip about you and me while they dare you and me to try to get in their business that may very well be like eating junk food.

Some people will say something on purpose to you and me to see what we will say.

Some people will see Jesus Christ living in you and me who don't have to say one word to them about Jesus.

Some church people will believe that you and I are not doing anything for Jesus if they don't see you and me bringing someone to church with us.

Some church people will believe that you and I are playing church, when they are judging you and me and playing God, who is the only one who knows all of your heart and all of my heart.

It's Best Not To

It's best not to talk about some things.

It's best not to listen to some things.

It's best not to look at some things.

It's best not to touch some things.

It's best not to go to some places.

It's best not to eat some foods.

It's best not to drink some liquids.

It's best not to talk too much.

It's best not to work too much.

It's best not to joke too much.

It's best not to sleep too much.

It's best not to disagreed too much.

It's best not to be quiet too much.

It's best not to laugh too much.

It's best not to exercise too much.

It's best not to think too much.

It's best not to write about some things.

It's best not to publish some things.

It's best not to judge anyone.

It's best not to argue.

It's best not to dwell on things.

It's best not to nag.

It's best not to complain.

It's best not to show favoritism.

It's best not to wear some clothes out in public places if they are seductive and draw the wrong kind of attention.

It's best not to stay up too late.

It's best not to pretend.

It's best not to start something and not finish it.

It's best not to say something and not really mean it.

It's best not to tell lies that will cause distrust.

It's best not to get angry if there is no self-control.

It's best not to have a dream if there is no perseverance.

It's best not to lay down and sleep on anger.

It's best not to spoil a child when prisons are not merciful.

It's best not to make a vow to the Lord if there is no following through on it.

It's best not to go to church if there is no desire to want to be like Jesus Christ.

It's best not to have been born if you blaspheme the Holy Spirit, who teaches all truth about Jesus Christ to spread around the world before Jesus Christ comes back again.

It's best not to blaspheme against the Holy Spirit, because that's the unpardonable sin God will not forgive.

It's best not to assume that God doesn't exist, when nature is a visual Bible every day and reveals that God does exist.

You Have to Use Good Judgment

If you are driving on the road and someone is driving on your bumper, you have to use good judgment to drive the speed limit and not speed up.

If you are talking to someone and the conversation is not good, you have to use good judgment to end the conversation in a nice way.

If you go into a grocery store and someone is standing in the middle of the lane with a grocery cart, you have to use good judgment and say excuse me to get around them.

If your life is threatened by someone who is very angry, you have to use good judgment to stay calm and be quiet, since that is a good thing to calm the person down.

If the doctor gives you some medicine to take and it causes you to feel bad, you have to use good judgment to stop taking the medicine and tell your doctor.

If you are on a monthly fixed income, you have to use good judgment and spend within your monthly budget.

If someone keeps hurting you, you have to use good judgment to keep your distance and stay away from that person.

If you don't like someone, you have to use good judgment and pray for that person to change for the better.

If you have more than one child, you have to use good judgment and not show favor over one more than the other.

If you are a leader in the church, you have to use good judgment and be humble before the church members who are God's children.

If you don't make a lot of money on your job, you have to use good judgment so you don't overspend your weekly or biweekly salary wage.

If someone doesn't like you, you have to use good judgment and be nice to that person who always needs the Lord.

If you talk to someone you don't know, you have to use good judgment and take your time to get to know that person who may or may not be good and honest.

If you believe that you are like Jesus Christ, you have to use good judgment to examine yourself and confess and repent of your sins for Jesus to forgive you and cleanse you so you can be like Him.

Attention

A lot of women love to show off their bodies to get some attention.

A lot of men love to show off their muscles to get some attention.

A lot of people are addicted to attention.

They've got to have some attention every day.

Attention can be a good thing and a bad thing.

It's always good for a man to give his attention to his wife and children.

It's always good for students to pay attention to their teachers.

It's always good for church folks to pay attention to their pastor's sermons, as long as they are in line with God's holy word.

When Jesus Christ lived here on earth, He got a lot of attention from people who wanted to be healed by Him.

Jesus deserved everybody's attention because He was the savior of the world.

Jesus was never addicted to getting a lot of attention because He didn't perform miracles to get a lot of attention from sinners.

There were times when Jesus wanted to be alone to pray to His Heavenly Father in heaven.

Today, a lot of people live their lives to get a lot of attention.

There are people who will commit terrible crimes to get a lot of attention so they can feel good about themselves.

The best attention to get is God's attention for loving Him and keeping His commandments.

You and I should always want to get God's attention and we will get it for believing in His Son, Jesus Christ, to be saved.

Getting God's attention is always the right kind of attention that we truly need.

A lot of people who love to get a lot of attention are getting the wrong kind of attention that makes them a victim of violence, abuse and even death.

When Jesus lived here on earth, He had a lot of good attention from many people who wanted to be near Him and get healed.

Jesus also got some bad attention from those who threatened Him because they were threatened by Him and wanted to kill Him for speaking the truth that they believed to be lies.

When Jesus lived here on earth, He never wanted any attention for Himself or to be considered great.

Jesus was always humble and paid good attention to all sinners who He gave up His life on the cross to save from being lost in sin.

Jesus Commands Us to Love Them

There are people who are murderers, and Jesus commands us to love them.

There are people who are thieves, and Jesus commands us to love them.

There are people who are homosexuals, and Jesus commands us to love them.

There are people who are child molesters, and Jesus commands us to love them.

There are people who are rapists, and Jesus commands us to love them.

There are people who are adulterers, and Jesus commands us to love them.

There are people who are cheaters, and Jesus commands us to love them.

There are people who are liars, and Jesus commands us to love them.

There are people who are proud, and Jesus commands us to love them.

There are people who are hateful, and Jesus commands us to love them.

There are people who are prejudiced, and Jesus commands us to love them.

There are people who are fornicators, and Jesus commands us to love them.

There are people who are blind, and Jesus commands us to love them.

There are people who are deaf, and Jesus commands us to love them.

There are people who have no arms, and Jesus commands us to love them.

There are people who are in wheelchairs, and Jesus commands us to love them.

There are people who have a learning disability, and Jesus commands us to love them.

There are people who are mentally ill, and Jesus commands us to love them.

There are people who are selfish, and Jesus commands us to love them.

There are people who are bad, and Jesus commands us to love them.

There are people who are troublemakers, and Jesus commands us to love them.

There are people who are envious, and Jesus commands us to love them.

There are people who are evil, and Jesus commands us to love them.

There are people who are hypocrites, and Jesus commands us to love them.

Jesus Christ, our Lord and Savior, loved all sinners but hated their sins when He lived here on earth without sin.

Jesus Christ gave up His life on the cross to save all men, women, boys and girls from being lost in our sins.

There are people who are atheists, and Jesus commands us to love them.

There are people who are greedy for worldly gain, and Jesus commands us to love them.

There are people who layup their treasures in this world, and Jesus commands us to love them.

There are people who are disrespectful, and Jesus commands us to love them.

There are people who are rude, and Jesus commands us to love them.

There are people who are mean, and Jesus commands us to love them.

There are people who are lazy, and Jesus commands us to love them.

There are people who don't love you and me, and Jesus commands us to love them.

Jesus loved people who didn't love Him when He lived here on earth.

There are people who show favoritism to certain people, and Jesus commands us to love them.

There are people who don't love themselves, and Jesus commands us to love them.

There are people who are foolish, and Jesus commands us to love them.

There are people who turned their backs on Jesus, and Jesus commands us to love them.

There are people who are pretenders in the church, and Jesus commands us to love them.

Jesus loves everybody but He hates their sins.

Sin is of the devil, who hates Jesus and everybody in this world.

Some People Believe

Some people believe that there is something wrong with you and me if we don't talk a lot like them.

Some people believe that there is something wrong with you and me if we don't smile a lot like them.

Some people believe that there is something wrong with you and me if we tell the truth about the bad things that we did in our lives.

Some people believe that there is something wrong with you and me if we don't eat what they eat.

Some people believe that there is something wrong with you and me if we don't dress like they dress.

Some people believe that there is something wrong with you and me if we don't believe what they believe.

Back in the Bible days, some people believed that something was wrong with Jesus Christ, who didn't want to use His power to overthrow the Roman government.

Back in the Bible days, some people believed that something was wrong with Jesus Christ because He didn't use his power to destroy His enemies who crucified Him.

Some people believe that something is wrong with you and me for being a Christian.

Some people believe that something is wrong with you and me if we are different from them.

Some church folks believe that something is wrong with you and me if we don't stand around and talk in God's holy sanctuary after the pastor's sermon is over.

You Can't Be Lazy

If you have some animals to take care of, you can't be lazy and sit around and do nothing for them.

If you get married, you can't be lazy and sit around and do nothing for your spouse and children.

If you want to prosper in life, you can't be lazy and sit around and do nothing.

If you want to make good things happen, you can't be lazy and sit around and do nothing.

If you want to bless other people's lives, you can't be lazy and sit around and do nothing.

If you want to get somewhere in life, you can't be lazy and sit around and do nothing.

If you want to be successful in life, you can't be lazy and sit around and do nothing.

If you give your life to the Lord, you can't be lazy and sit around and do nothing for the Lord.

Even wicked people are not lazy on doing evil things that many of them do greatly prosper from because of not sitting around and doing nothing, even though it's wrong to do evil works.

Help Me to Keep My Eyes on You

Help me to keep my eyes on You, O Lord.

I don't want to keep my eyes on people's mistakes.

Help me to keep my eyes on You, O Lord.

I don't want to keep my eyes on people's flaws.

Help me to keep my eyes on You, O Lord.

I don't want to keep my eyes on people's bad habits.

Help me to keep my eyes on You, O Lord.

I don't want to keep my eyes on people's imperfections.

Help me to keep my eyes on You, O Lord.

I don't want to keep my eyes on people's failures.

Help me to keep my eyes on You, O Lord.

I don't want to keep my eyes on people's weaknesses.

Help me to keep my eyes on You, O Lord.

I don't want to keep my eyes on people's prejudices.

Help me to keep my eyes on You, O Lord.

I don't want to keep my eyes on people's misfortunes.

Help me to keep my eyes on You, O Lord.

I don't want to keep my eyes on people's riches and wealth.

Help me to keep my eyes on You, O Lord.

I don't want to keep my eyes on people's achievements.

Help me to keep my eyes on You, O Lord.

I don't want to keep my eyes on people's wrongdoings.

Help me to keep my eyes on You, O Lord.

I don't want to keep my eyes on people's sins.

I want to keep my eyes on You, O Lord, who are right about every word that You say.

I want to keep my eyes on You, O Lord, who are right about everything that You do.

I don't want to keep my eyes on people who can get wealth and lose their wealth.

I don't want to keep my eyes on people who can be educated fools.

I don't want to keep my eyes on people can be hypocrites in the church.

I want to keep my eyes on You, O Lord, who is the head of the church to separate the wheat from the tares.

I want to keep my eyes on You, O Lord.

I don't want to keep my eyes on me, who has sins to confess and repent unto You.

Imaginary

Many people believe that God is imaginary, like an imaginary book that lacks the real truth.

God is not imaginary, God is real like the invisible air that we breathe in and out of our noses.

Many people will think an imaginary thing and get it published and produced into a movie, even though it's not based on a true story.

The Bible is a true story book for you and me to read about God, who is not imaginary and is all-powerful beyond a bestselling imaginary book.

Many children believe that an imaginary book is real and it makes them feel powerful like they can conquer anything.

We can imagine things in our minds that are not real and not true, but God is real and true in His holy word and in our lives when we believe in His Son, Jesus Christ, who many people believe to be imaginary in the Bible.

If imaginary things can cause many people to feel good about themselves, then what about God who is forever real and gives you an me real, true joy to make us feel so good about loving and obeying Him?

Many people will imagine things that are not real and will talk about them and spread them around like they are real.

The gospel of Jesus Christ is real, good news to hear about in a pastor's sermon.

The gospel of Jesus Christ is real, good news for a Sabbath school teacher to teach.

The gospel of Jesus Christ is real, good news for every child of God to spread around beyond the imaginary things that are temporary and will one day pass away.

There is no real life in imaginary things, but God is real and gives us real life and a real free will to choose to live with our minds stayed on Him who is forever real or choose to live with our minds stayed on imaginary things that have no real heaven to put us in.

The Truth Will Never Retire

The truth will never age and get old, because the truth will stay young while you and I age if it's in the Lord's will.

Many people have aged, gotten old and retired from their jobs.

Many people have retired from the military.

Many politicians have retired from the White House.

The truth will never age, grow old and retire from the courtrooms, but judges will retire from the courtrooms.

The truth will never age, grow old and retire from the Bible where God's truth is forever and ever young.

The truth will never age, grow old and retire from the church, but many pastors will age, get old and retire from preaching the truth of God in the church.

Many school teachers will age, get old and retire from teaching many truths to their students.

Many publishers will age, get old and retire from publishing many books of many authors' truths.

The truth will never age, get old and retire.

The truth is young and every generation will learn the truth, especially about God's love to all the world through His Son, Jesus Christ, who is the everlasting truth.

The truth will never age, get old and retire and it will not die, because Jesus Christ is the origin of truth and life eternal so the truth can be forever young.

Many astronauts have aged, gotten old, and retired from going into outer space to discover more truths about other galaxies and black holes in outer space, where the truth of God's creation is forever young.

The truth will never age, get old and retire in this old sinful world where everything gets old under the sun except the truth.

Many movie stars will age, get old and retire from making some of their movies based on a true story, but the truth will never age, get old and retire from the TV screen where the daily news broadcasts the truth.

The truth will never age, get old and retired from working for Jesus Christ, who gave God's love and truth to all the world to know that there is a true, living God who will never change His truth to a lie.

God is the everlasting truth and will never age, get old and retire from His holy throne in heaven.

The Earth is God's footstool for God to step down on earth with His truth and love.

Live a Long Life

Many people live a long life because they treat everybody right.

Many people live a long life because they take good care of themselves.

Many people live a long life because they eat right.

Many people live a long life because they drink the right liquids.

Many people live a long life because they live right.

Many people live a long life because they learn from their mistakes and do good things.

Many people live a long life because they think on good, positive things.

Many people live a long life because they stay out of trouble.

Many people live a long life because they don't overwork themselves.

Many people live a long life because they exercise their body.

Many people live a long life because they talk right.

Many people live a long life because they are good.

Many people live a long life because they are cheerful.

Many people live a long life because they are humble.

Many people live a long life because they are giving.

Many people live a long life because they are loving.

Many people live a long life because they are wise.

Many people live a long life because they are selfless.

Many people live a long life because they are healthy.

Many people live a long life because they get a good night's sleep.

Many people live a long life because they love Jesus and keep His commandments.

Many people live a long life because they pray to God without ceasing.

Many people live a long life because they study their Bible and live by it every day.

Choosing to live right unto God can surely give us a long life to live, but some God-fearing people will die young because only God truly knows why He allows their lives to be shortened when we don't have the slightest clue.

Overcome

It's the Lord who gives us all the strength to overcome bad things in our lives.

Many people overcome bad things in their lives and they won't acknowledge that the Lord helped them to overcome those bad things in their lives.

Many people will say, "I overcome the bad things," when they don't realize that it's the Lord who allows them to overcome those bad things.

All good things are from the Lord, who helps us all to overcome the bad things in our lives.

The devil will try his best to keep anyone from overcoming any bad thing.

The devil loves to cause us to be defeated by the bad things in our lives.

You and I don't have any strength on our own to overcome anything.

Many people will believe that they overcome bad things on their own with their own strength, but that is no match for the devil, who will overpower us if the Lord allows him to do so.

Our strength comes from the Lord, even though many people don't believe it and will live their lives like they can overcome anything that comes their way.

Can Come and Go

Money can come and money can go into a negative balance in a checking account.

Parties can come and parties can go into getting some injuries from a collapsed balcony.

Food can come and food can go out of the refrigerator and cabinets and leave them empty.

A hurricane can come and can go, leaving behind water, floods and ruined houses.

Guns can come and guns can go into the hands of children, the mentally ill and criminals.

Peace can come and peace can go into violence and war.

Love can come and love can go into divorce and hate.

Education can come and go into foolishness.

Wealth can come and go into poverty.

Prosperity can come and go into oppression.

Our words can come and go into only hot air.

Words can come and can go into good actions or bad actions.

Good health can come and go into bad eating habits and bad living habits.

We can come to church and can go out of the church being no different from the way that we went in.

We can come to Jesus Christ and can go away from Jesus if we don't give Jesus all of our hearts.

We can come to the truth of God's holy word and can go away from the truth of God's holy word if we don't live by it.

God has Plenty of His

God has plenty of His mercy to give to everybody in this world.

God has plenty of His grace to give to everybody in this world.

God has plenty of His blessings to give to everybody in this world.

God has plenty of His salvation to give to everybody who believes in his son, Jesus Christ.

God has plenty of His hope to give to everybody who has hope in his Son, Jesus Christ.

God has plenty of His faith to give to everybody who has faith and his Son, Jesus Christ.

God has plenty of His purpose to give to everybody who puts their trust in his Son, Jesus Christ.

God has plenty of His strength to give to everybody who prays to his Son, Jesus Christ, for strength.

God has plenty of His truth to give to everybody who wants to live by the truth that is his Son, Jesus Christ, who the Bible's truth is all about to set everybody free.

God has plenty of His love to give to everybody who denies themselves and picks up their crosses to follow His Son, Jesus Christ, out of their love for Him.

God has plenty of His goodness to give to everybody to repent of their sins unto his Son, Jesus Christ.

God has plenty of His spiritual gifts to give to everybody to use to minister good works in His son, Jesus Christ.

God has plenty of His respect to give to everybody to not show respect of persons, because His Son, Jesus Christ, loves everybody the same and will save everybody from their sins.

God has plenty of His cheer to give to everybody, too especially be a cheerful giver of returning a faithful tithes and offerings unto his son, Jesus Christ.

God has plenty of His fruit of the Holy Spirit to give to everybody who chooses to love and obey His Son, Jesus Christ, every day.

God has plenty of His forgiveness to give to everybody who confesses and repents of their sins unto his Son, Jesus Christ.

God has plenty of His everlasting life to give to everybody who believes in his Son, Jesus Christ, who is coming back again to give eternal life to all of God's righteous children, including you and me if we are saved in His Son, Jesus Christ.

God has plenty of His spiritual things to give to everybody for living by faith and His Son, Jesus Christ, when living by eyesight is plenty of unbelief.

God has plenty of His healing to give to everybody who is broken in sin, for only His Son, Jesus Christ, to make us spiritually well and also heal our minds and bodies.

Living to be Number One

Wanting to be number one has caused many people to ruin themselves.

Wanting to be number one has caused many people to ruin other people's lives.

Wanting to be number one has caused many people to lose everything they had.

Wanting to be number one has caused many people to lose good friends.

Wanting to be number one has caused many people to hurt their loved ones.

Wanting to be number one has caused many people to lie about other people.

Wanting to be number one has caused many people to make other people sick.

Wanting to be number one in the church has caused many people to divide the church.

Wanting to be number one in the church has caused many people to leave the church.

Wanting to be number one in the church has caused many people to make enemies in the church.

Wanting to be number one in the church has caused many people to ruin their own walk with Jesus Christ.

Wanting to be number one has caused Lucifer and his angels to be cast out of heaven.

To Make Enemies

It's much better to make enemies for doing the Lord's will than to make enemies for doing bad things.

Making enemies for living right unto the Lord will cause the holy Angels to greatly protect you and me from our enemies.

To make enemies for being a Christian will cause the Lord to be joyful and rejoice.

It's much better to make enemies for believing in Jesus Christ than to make enemies for doing evil things.

Murderers will make enemies for killing people, but a Christian can make enemies for winning souls to Jesus Christ.

A liar will make enemies for lying to people, but a Christian can make enemies for telling the Bible's truth to people.

A gossiper will make enemies for talking bad about people behind their backs, but a Christian can make enemies for calling people's sins out by their right names.

To make enemies for being a witness of Jesus Christ will cause the holy angels to come to our rescue faster than the speed of light.

To make enemies for not denying Jesus Christ before the world will cause God to give you and me His favor from heaven above.

It's much better to make enemies for being like Jesus Christ than to make enemies for being like the devil.

Wicked people will cause God to be their enemy sooner or later and He will make them reap what they sow.

Only a fool would make God his enemy, because no one can outsmart God or outdo God and only a fool would believe that he or she can do that.

To make enemies for being a Christian will cause God to reveal much more of His presence to you and me, even if we have to face death, our worst enemy that Jesus Christ got the victory over to give you and me eternal life.

We are Not
Our Own Worst Enemy

No one is their worst enemy, because death is our worst enemy.

As long as we are alive, we can choose to be a good friend to ourselves and most of all we can choose to be a good friend to the Lord.

Death is our worst enemy because when we die, we can't make any more choices to choose to be our worst enemy or choose to be a good friend to ourselves.

When we die, we have no conscious mind to believe that we are our worst enemy, and that means nothing at all in the grave where death is our worst enemy.

The devil wants you to believe that you are your own worst enemy, but you have a free will to choose to be a good friend to yourself by taking good care of yourself if you are able to take care of yourself.

God wants you and me to love Him.

God wants us to love our neighbors and God wants you and me to love ourselves so that we can choose to do what we can choose to do in the land of the living.

Our worst enemy is death, which gets rid of all of our life choices and activities and gives us no more conscious mind to choose to believe the truth or believe lies.

Death is our worst enemy and permanently separates us from making life choices that God gave us a free will to do.

God didn't create us to be our worst enemy.

The devil deceives many people and makes them believe that they are their worst enemy so that they will take their own lives, but they had a free will to choose life over death.

We are not our own worst enemy because if that was true, the devil would have power over our choices and then we really would be our own worst enemy.

God wonderfully made us to not be our worst enemy.

God gave us all a free will to choose and the devil can't take that away from us.

We can choose to love ourselves and be a good friend to ourselves and not be our own worst enemy.

We can choose to believe that we are not our own worst enemy because Jesus made a way for you and me to escape the devil's overpowering temptations.

We can come to Jesus, who is our Lord and Savior and our best friend, who will help us to be a good friend to Him and to ourselves who have a free will to choose not to be our own worst enemy.

Death is our worst enemy because death proves that to us if we get very sick and feel like we will die.

Death is our worst enemy and death proves that to us if our loved ones die.

Death is our worst enemy and death proves that to us if our life is in great danger.

Death is our worst enemy and death proves that to us in the graveyards.

We are not our own worst enemy because God created us in His image, and the devil can't take that away from us and make us choose to be our worst enemy.

None of God's prophets of old were their own worst enemy, because death was their worst enemy.

Elijah knew this and ran away from Jezebel, who wanted to kill him.

Death was Jesus' worst enemy, because death separated Jesus from God, who raised Jesus from the dead and gave Him the victory over death in the grave.

If we all truly were our own worst enemy, then we would have nothing worthwhile to live for or feel good about choosing to make good choices in our lives.

The Lord Jesus Christ was never His own worst enemy and that proves to us that we are not our own worst enemy either.

Jesus never gave in to that lie of being his own worst enemy.

Only the devil is his own worst enemy and will one day burn in hell a lot longer than his fallen angels and human agents who will burn up into ashes like the Bible says in Malachi 4:3.

Many People Don't Want To

Many people don't want to hear anything about God, because many people are holding grudges against God because He didn't spare the life of their loved ones.

Many people don't want to talk about God, who they believe didn't answer their prayers even though God always knows what is best for everyone even if they don't see it.

Many people don't want to talk to you and me because we believe in God's Son, Jesus Christ.

They believe that we are wasting our time going to church to worship the Lord, who they believed to have wasted their time because He didn't give them what they want, even though the Lord knows they don't need what they want.

Many people don't want to have anything to do with you and me because we are being like Jesus Christ, and that causes the demons to tremble in them when they see you and me being strong in the Lord and facing up to them with the love of God.

There are so-called Christians who don't want to be around you and me because we don't kiss-up to their proud ways.

There are so-called Christians who don't want to talk to you and me because we aren't in their circle of friends.

There are so-called Christians who don't want to look at you and me because we are not like them in their high-minded ways.

They want to look down on you and me like they are God in heaven.

Many people don't want to go to church because of so-called Christians who look at them like they don't belong in the church.

Many people don't want to have anything to do with the Lord Jesus Christ because they see so-called Christians arguing with one another and some of them gossiping about one another.

Many people don't want to believe in Jesus Christ because of so-called Christians living by eyesight for the material things that they see and want to get in this world.

Many so-called Christians live their lives like Jesus doesn't exist, and many Christians don't want to believe that having faith in Jesus can move mountains.

Will Always Last

Doing what is right in the home will always last.

Doing what is right in the neighborhood will always last.

Doing what is right in the community will always last.

Doing what is right on the job will always last.

Doing what is right in the schools will always last.

Doing what is right in the government will always last.

Doing what is right on the streets will always last.

Doing what is right in the marriage will always last.

Doing what is right in the city will always last.

Doing what is right in the country will always last.

Doing what is right in the nation will always last.

Doing what is right in the church will always last.

Doing what is right by God will always last.

Doing what is wrong won't always last.

Doing what is wrong will sooner or later come to an end.

Doing what is right will get better and better.

Doing what is wrong will get worse and worse.

Doing what is right in your heart will always last.

Doing what is right by God's holy word will always last.

Doing what is right in the truth will always last.

Doing what is right in your life will always last.

Doing what is right in God's way of doing things will always last.

We are Ignorant and Do Not Know

We are ignorant and do not know what a day will bring us.

We are ignorant and do not know what can happen next.

We are ignorant and do not know our unseen sins.

We are ignorant and do not know how the Lord will bless us.

We are ignorant and do not know all the spiritual things of God.

We are ignorant and do not know what is going on while we sleep and have dreams all night long.

We are ignorant and do not know what is ahead of us.

We are ignorant and do not know if we will live to see another day.

We are ignorant and do not know how many angels are camped around us.

We are ignorant and do not know all who will enter into heaven.

We are ignorant and do not know who is praying for us.

We are ignorant and do not know who sees Jesus in us.

We are ignorant and do not know who we have greatly touched with our testimonies about what Jesus brought us through.

We are ignorant and do not know every scripture in the Bible.

We are ignorant and do not always know what we will say.

We are ignorant and do not always know what we will do.

We are ignorant and do not always know who the Lord can use to help us.

We are ignorant and do not always know who the Lord can greatly bless.

We are ignorant and do not always know who we have encouraged to do the Lord's will by our living example.

The most Bible knowledgeable Christians are ignorant and do not always know a wheat from a tare.

The most loving and obedient Christians are ignorant and do not always know who is truly saved in Jesus Christ.

The most outstanding Christians are ignorant and do not always know if they're calling in Jesus is very sure, especially when their faith is tested to the maximum strength.

But It's Not Good

It's good to get an education, but it's not good to put it above the Lord.

It's good to prosper, but it's not good to put it above the Lord.

It's good to be successful, but it's not good to put it above the Lord.

It's good to make achievements, but it's not good to put them above the Lord.

It's good to be in good health, but it's not good to put that above the Lord.

It's good to be brilliant, but it's not good to put it above the Lord.

It's good to be intelligent, but it's not good to put it above the Lord.

It's good to be rich, but it's not good to put it above the Lord.

The Lord gives good things and the Lord can take them away.

Everything belongs to the Lord, who shows no respect of persons with His blessings.

It's good to do good things, but it's not good to put them above the Lord.

It's good to do great things, but it's not good to put them above the Lord.

All good things are from the Lord, who is good all the time to you and me who are not always good to the Lord.

It's good to love everybody, but it's not good to put anyone above the Lord.

It's good to have talents, but it's not good to put them above the Lord.

It's good to have skills, but it's not good to put them above the Lord.

It's good to have spiritual gifts, but it's not good to put them above the Lord.

The Lord giveth and the Lord can take it away if we put anything above Him who owns everyone and everything.

It's good to have a job, but it's not good to put it above the Lord, who makes us able to work.

It's good to be in the military, but it's not good to put it above the Lord.

It's good to look beautiful, but it's not good to put it above the Lord.

It's good to have muscles, but it's not good to put it above the Lord.

The Lord giveth and can take it away.

I Greatly Miss My Mom

I greatly miss my mom.

A million teardrops can't define my grief.

My heart is like one million pieces of broken glass.

I greatly miss my mom.

A big part of my life is missing.

The rest of my days are wounded.

I greatly miss my mom.

My growing up life can never take away my childhood mentality toward my mom.

The grave can never erase my mom from my memory, where I see her loving and obeying Jesus Christ.

I greatly miss my mom.

My mother was a mother and father who never abandoned me.

Like a warm blanket, my mom kept me warm in her love, even through the cold winter seasons of my life.

I greatly miss my mom, who I want to see again when Jesus Christ comes back.

All the good spoken words about my mom are only like a bubble that bursts compared to Jesus giving my mom eternal life when He comes back again.

I greatly miss my mom.

She chose to give me life, which she didn't have to do.

My mom didn't let poverty handicap her from raising me up to choose my destiny.

I greatly miss my mom.

Jesus had appointed my mom to give me a timely birth in a world of many people dying before their time for being too wicked.

I greatly miss my mom, but her death can never separate her from the love of my Lord and Savior Jesus Christ, who she loved, and I witnessed that love when my mom was in my life.

My mom's love was perfect to me and I saw Jesus in my mom from my childhood days to my grown-up days.

My mom could have chosen to be a bad mom to me, but she chose to be a good mom to me instead.

My mom showed me how to love people for who they are, even before I set foot in the church to hear about Jesus.

I surely know today that my mom's love was truly next to the love of Jesus Christ.

I greatly miss my mom.

The years that my mom have been departed from me are like no years have passed by when I see my mom in my mind.

She lived for Jesus and praised His holy name.

My mom was no better than anyone else's mom, but I am so glad that she loved me when my father wasn't in my life.

Can't Overpower

Palm readers can't overpower God's holy word that is all truth to always predict what will happen to you and me if we live right onto the Lord or don't live right onto the Lord.

Witches can't overpower God's holy word that is all truth to keep you and me safe from the devil's deceptive lies.

Horoscopes can't overpower God's holy word that is all truth to always predict the character of everyone in this world.

No one in this world can overpower God's holy word that is all truth to set everyone free from the devil's lies.

The devil can't overpower God's holy word that is all truth to always let us know the tricks of the devil.

The devil can't overpower God's holy word that is all truth against the devil's temptations that can't overpower you and me if we're living by God's holy word every day.

Luck can't overpower God's holy word that is all truth and predicts everything good or bad that we don't see coming our way.

Mysterious things can't overpower God's holy word that is all truth to solve the deepest mysteries in this world.

Nothing in this world can overpower God's holy word that is all truth to predict the destiny of all human beings.

Eternally Brighter Than

God is eternally brighter than one trillion suns, which seem dark compared to God.

God shines very bright throughout the heavens and other worlds.

One day in the new earth there won't be any night, because God will greatly shine His eternal light twenty-four hours around the clock.

God will fill the new earth with His eternal light for you and me to have no need to lay down and sleep.

God's eternal light will energize our lives forever and ever in the new Jerusalem holy city that God will fill with His eternal light shining brighter than all the stars in all the universes that He created.

God the father, the Son, and the Holy Spirit give their eternal light to all the angels in heaven to shine bright throughout the heavens.

When Jesus Christ comes back again, He will give you and me God's eternal light to shine through our eternal bodies that Jesus will give to us for being saved in Him.

When Jesus comes back again, He will shine brighter than one trillion suns and the living wicked will fall dead from the brightness of Jesus Christ.

The dead in Jesus Christ will rise in the eternal light of God and the righteous living will look into the brightness of Jesus and be changed to immortality in the twinkling of an eye.

God is eternally brighter than one trillion nuclear bombs exploding that look dark when compared to God's eternal bright light.

Don't Let

If your husband is not doing right, don't let your husband keep you from going to heaven.

If your wife is not doing right, don't let your wife keep you from going to heaven.

If your friends are not doing right, don't let your friends keep you from going to heaven.

If your neighbors are not doing right, don't let your neighbors keep you from going to heaven.

If your children are not doing right, don't let your children keep you from going to heaven.

If your father is not doing right, don't let your father keep you from going to heaven.

If your mother is not doing right, don't let your mother keep you from going to heaven.

If your pastor is not doing right, don't let your pastor keep you from going to heaven.

Don't let anybody keep you from going to heaven with Jesus Christ when He comes back again to take you and me to heaven for being saved in Him.

If your brothers are not doing right, don't let your brothers keep you from going to heaven.

If your kinfolks are not doing right, don't let your kinfolks keep you from going to heaven where you and I will have countless spiritual kinfolks throughout the heavens.

Don't let yourself keep you from going to heaven.

Believe in Jesus Christ and He will save you from being lost in yourself who has sins to confess and repent unto the Lord, who is perfect without sin over you and me.

Don't let yourself keep you from going to heaven.

Live your life doing God's holy will and not your will that will keep you from going to heaven when Jesus comes back again on the clouds of glory.

Don't let anything in this world keep you from going to heaven.

This whole world will one day pass away and will take you and me away with it to hell if we are lost in our sins and miss out on heaven forever and ever.

God is a Big-Time God

God is a big-time God who is all-present for no time to exist in him.

God is a big-time God who created the heavens and earth.

God is a big-time God who gave us His only begotten Son to save us from our sins.

God is a big-time God who will give us eternal life through His Son, Jesus Christ.

God is a big-time God who cannot lie to you and me.

God is a big-time God who cannot fail you and me.

God is a big-time God who is everywhere at the same time.

God is a big-time God who the devil is no match for at anytime, anywhere.

God is a big-time God above the small-time sinful world.

God is a big-time God above small-time sinners saved through God's grace.

God is a big-time God who is holy, righteous and perfect.

God is a big-time God who is all-seeing, all-knowing and all-powerful.

God is a big-time God who is love and all-powerful and forever and ever.

God is a big-time God above small-minded atheists who believe that there is no God.

God is a big-time God above anyone who believes they are self-made, because it's God who can make anyone get rich and make anyone live in poverty.

God is a big-time God who loves small-time sinners like you and me through His Son, Jesus Christ, who was small-time to those who crucified Him on the cross.

Those Pharisees and Roman soldiers believed that they were big-time to Jesus, who humbled himself unto death that was small-time to Jesus when He rose from the dead.

Rich people are big-time in the eyes of many poor people every day, but God is a big-time God above the rich and famous.

They are truly poor to God, who has streets made of pure gold that you and I will walk on when Jesus Christ comes back again to take us to heaven for being saved in Him, who is big-time to all the angels in heaven and big-time to other worlds that He created.

We Live in a World Where

We live in a world where little children are getting shot and killed as if their life means nothing.

We live in a world where many police officers are eager to beat up and kill anyone who makes them angry, and they don't care if you are young or old or male or female.

We live in a world where many parents don't secure their guns and keep them away from their children, who behave like criminals because their parents don't teach them right from wrong.

We live in a world where God is not honored in many homes and they break down in criminal activities.

We live in a world where many people are killing people in their own race and feeling good about it, while hating on people of another race for killing people who look different.

We live in a world where many Christians will act surprised to see so much wickedness in these last days that the Bible predicted.

Many Christians don't study their Bible to know what is going on in this world that will one day pass away like the Bible says.

Our Mind is Like the Open-Wide Sky

Our mind is like the open wide sky for the sunlight of God's holy word to shine through our minds.

Our mind is like the open-wide sky for the full white moonlight of God's love to glow in our mind.

Our mind is like the open-wide sky for all of the stars of God's truth to sparkle in our mind.

Our mind is like the open-wide sky for the rain of disappointments to fall down in our mind.

Our mind is like the open-wide sky for the fog of doubt to enter into our mind.

Our mind is like the open-wide sky for the clouds of confusion to enter into our mind.

Our mind just like the open-wide sky for the heatwave of trouble to enter into our mind.

Our mind is like the open-wide sky for the snow blizzard of lies to enter into our mind.

Our mind is like the open-wide sky for the freezing cold weather of not trusting God to enter into our mind.

Our mind is like the open-wide sky for the gentle warm breeze of God's peace to enter into our mind.

Our mind is like the open-wide sky for the fresh air of God's strength to enter into our mind.

Our mind is like the open-wide sky for the hell of God's judgment to enter into our mind.

Our mind is like the open-wide sky that anything can fall through, but only God can command it all to open our minds so we repent unto His Son, Jesus Christ, in love and obey Him.

On the Rise

Governments are changing laws that are on the rise.

Corruption is on the rise.

Deception is on the rise.

Viruses are on the rise.

Diseases are on the rise.

Hurricanes are on the rise.

Tornadoes are on the rise.

Floods are on the rise.

Wildfires are on the rise.

Snow blizzards are on the rise.

Political strife is on the rise.

Murders are on the rise.

Protests are on the rise.

Wars are on the rise.

Childhood abuse is on the rise.

Missing people are on the rise.

Human trafficking is on the rise.

Earthquakes are on the rise.

Volcanic eruptions are on the rise.

Heatwaves are on the rise.

Divorces are on the rise.

Bullying is on the rise.

Suicides are on the rise.

Atheism is on the rise.

Spiritualism is on the rise.

Adultery is on the rise.

Same-sex marriages are on the rise.

Childbirth out of wedlock is on the rise.

Brutality is on the rise.

Theft is on the rise.

False accusers are on the rise.

Technology is on the rise.

Dreamers are on the rise.

Inventions are on the rise.

Mysteries are on the rise.

Poverty is on the rise.

Greed is on the rise.

Pride is on the rise.

Animal abuse is on the rise.

Foolishness is on the rise.

Scoffers are on the rise.

Leaving the church is on the rise.

Denying Jesus Christ is on the rise.

Turning away from Jesus is on the rise.

Wisdom Doesn't Come With

Wisdom doesn't come with iPhones.

Wisdom doesn't come with computers.

Wisdom doesn't come with reading books.

Wisdom doesn't come with technology.

Wisdom doesn't come with science.

Wisdom doesn't come with success.

Wisdom doesn't come with education.

Many educated people make bad choices.

Wisdom doesn't come with marriage.

Many married couples make bad choices.

Wisdom doesn't come with age.

Many old people make bad choices.

Wisdom doesn't come with money.

Many people will get in debt.

Wisdom doesn't come with wealth.

Many people are wealthy and make bad choices.

Wisdom doesn't come with big muscles.

Many strong men make bad choices.

Wisdom doesn't come with beauty.

Many beautiful women make bad choices.

Wisdom doesn't come with having children.

Many parents make bad choices.

Wisdom comes with fearing God and keeping His Commandments.

Wisdom doesn't come with going to church.

Many people go to church and make bad choices.

Wisdom comes with believing in Jesus Christ.

Wisdom doesn't come with having skills.

Many people have skills and make bad choices.

Wisdom doesn't come with talents.

Many people have a lot of talents and make bad choices.

Wisdom comes with repenting of our sins and living a renewed life unto Jesus Christ.

O Lord, You are With Me

O Lord, You are with me even when my mind is cloudy like a cloudy day.

O Lord, You are with me, even when my thoughts are lost like being lost in a forest.

O Lord, You are with me, even when my heart is shipwrecked like a ship banging up on the rocky seashore.

O Lord, You are with me, even when my day is bad like a bad dog wanting to bite someone.

O Lord, You are with me, even when I don't feel Your presence that is all around me.

O Lord, You are with me, even when I don't see my way out of a bad situation that You already worked out for me, O Lord.

O Lord, You are with me, even when my enemies make me look bad when You will make me look good in Your own time, Lord.

O Lord, You are with me, even when hard times come my way when You will let me know that You are with me.

O Lord, You are with me, even when I feel uncertain that You, O Lord, can make certain for me to live out my life doing Your holy will.

O Lord, You are with me even when I get misunderstood, that You, O Lord, will make clear for me to be a blessing to anyone who sees You in me, O Lord.

It Takes Humility to Ask for Help

It takes humility to ask for help if we need help.

Many people are too proud to ask for help that they need.

There are people who are too proud to ask the Lord to help them.

They believe they don't need the Lord's help.

There are people who would rather starve before they ask for help.

There are people who would rather get sick before they ask for help.

There are people who would rather be homeless before they ask for help.

There are people who would rather die before they ask for help.

It takes humility to ask for help when we need help.

Asking for help is showing that we are wise.

Asking for help is showing that we don't believe that we are better than others.

Asking for help is showing that we can't do it all on our own.

We can always ask the Lord to help us, because the Lord will do this on his time which is always being on time.

We can always ask the Lord to help us to say the right words.

We can always ask the Lord to help us do what is right.

It takes humility to ask for help.

We should not be too proud to ask anyone to help us if we need their help to pick us up if we fall down and hurt ourselves.

We all need help in some kind of way and the Lord can use anyone to help us, regardless of the color of their skin.

It takes humility to ask for help, and pride will take us to a fall for the Lord to help us humble ourselves into him.

We Can't Age Out Sin

We can't age out sin.

Sin will stick with us until we grow old and die.

There are a lot of old sinners, as well as a lot of young sinners.

We can't age out sin because we must confess and repent of those sins unto the Lord Jesus Christ.

The Lord is the only one who can cleanse us of our sins.

Getting old can't cleanse us of our sins.

We can't age out sin no matter how wise we are.

We can't age out sin no matter how much we learn from our mistakes.

We can't age out sin no matter how experienced we are in life.

We can't age out sin, because sins can get larger in number as we get older.

We can't age out sin, because sins can get a stronger hold on us as we get older.

We can't age out sin, because the devil can tempt us more and more as we get older.

What is worse than a young fool is an old fool.

We can't age out sin because only Jesus Christ can cleanse us of our sins.

We must confess and repent of our sins unto the Lord Jesus Christ who can cleanse anyone of their sins no matter how old they are.

We can't age out sin no matter how mature we are.

We can't age out sin no matter how much we know.

The devil will tempt the young, middle-aged, and the old to sin against God.

No one in this world can age out sin.

Many old people are sinning against God.

Many old people are living in their sins.

Many old people have died being lost in their sins.

Whether you are young, middle-aged or old sinners, the oldest people in this world can't age out sin, because only Jesus Christ can cleanse us of our sins.

No one can get too old not to sin against God.

No matter how long we live, there are seen and unseen sins in our lives that we can't age out of.

Growing old has no power to cleanse us from our sins, only Jesus Christ can do that.

Many People are Getting Killed Every Day

Many people are getting killed every day like it's no big deal.

Many people are getting killed every day like there's nothing to it.

Many people are getting killed every day like it's a normal way of life.

Many people are getting killed every day like it's the right thing to do.

Many people are getting killed every day like it's a business to run.

Many people are getting killed every day like it's not insane to do.

Many people are getting killed every day like cows being slaughtered.

Many people are getting killed every day like eating food.

Many people are getting killed every day like breathing air in and out of our nostrils.

Many people are getting killed every day like wearing clothes.

Many people are getting killed every day like brushing our teeth.

Many people are getting killed every day like looking in the mirror.

The Lord says, "Thou shalt not kill," but natural disasters kill many people.

The Lord says, "Thou shall kill," but earthquakes kill many people.

Death will try to kill us in one way or another.

Our only hope is in the Lord to keep us alive if it's in His will for you and me to even live another day.

Many people are killed every day and we can be so numb to it.

The Lord, who is in control of all things, allows many people to be killed every day and His reasons are always right, no matter how we feel about many people getting killed every day.

We can't question the Lord about what He allows to happen in this world day after day.

The Lord always knows what is best, whether it's to let us live a long life or a short life.

We can be so far off the mark that it's up to the Lord to give life and take it away.

Who are we to have the nerve to break bad with the Lord if we lose a loved one, who also belongs to the Lord and has to answer to Him on the way to heaven or hell?

Many people are getting killed every day, but the Lord is not slack and will seal all of His righteous children to go to heaven when He comes back again.

On that Highway to Heaven

I dreamed about a trailer that was hooked up to a car.

On top of the trailer was a red sofa pillow seat with white flowers painted on it.

There was also a suit that looked like it had just been picked up from the cleaners.

The suit was still on the hanger and was covered in plastic.

Then the scene in my dream changed to an old tall tree that I was standing beside and when I dug my finger into the tree, it was made of flesh like meat.

I tasted the meat and it tasted like beef that had been cooked.

The scene in my dream changed again and I saw two young black men walking into an apartment complex.

One of the black men spoke to me as he was walking into the apartment.

The scene in my dream changed again and I was laying down on top of a black mattress with the red sofa pillow seat.

The scene in my dream changed again and I was inside of a go-kart going down a local road with the red sofa pillow on top of the go-kart that got its power from the wind so it could roll down the road.

As I was in the go-kart rolling down the local road, I went through a red light because I couldn't stop.

The go-kart kept on rolling faster, and I went through another red light at the next intersection.

I came to a little store that the go-kart rolled into, and I ended up in a small bedroom and saw a picture of an old black man wearing glasses.

The go-kart rolled back out of the bedroom and I saw a local road leading me onto a highway.

The go-kart took me to a terminal where I had to get checked in before I could get onto the highway.

At the terminal, the go-kart rolled by a black woman in a blue uniform.

She had a big smile on her face as I roll by her in the go-kart.

I rolled up to a booth and then I saw another black woman standing far off from me and near to the highway road sign.

I also saw a busload of white and black children heading toward the highway.

The children were piled up on a small bus with their arms hanging out the windows.

I stood by and looked at the school bus going onto the highway; I couldn't go any farther.

The Lord reminded me that I broke the law by going through the red lights.

The Lord let me know, even in my dream, that there won't be any lawbreakers going to heaven.

Jesus says, "If you love me you will keep my Commandments."

Little children who don't know right from wrong will go to heaven, but we adults know a lot of right from wrong and will not go to heaven if we break God's law.

If we know to do right and don't do it, we sin against God, whose law is holy, righteous and perfect.

There won't be any lawbreakers in heaven.

If we make it to heaven when Jesus comes back, we will get food from the tree of life that is filled with fruits.

That old tree that was made of meat in my dream will not be in heaven.

We will not be eating meat in heaven.

God's holy law and God's health message are from the beginning of life on earth to set a steady pace for us on that highway to heaven.

For Our Good

The Lord will work things out for our good, if we learn from our mistakes and wait on the Lord to give us what we need.

The Lord will work things out for our good, if we are faithful to the Lord and trust Him even when things look not so sure in our lives.

The Lord will work things out for our good, if we stay in prayer unto Him even if it takes years and years for the Lord to answer our prayers because the Lord will answer everything on time.

The Lord will work things out for our good, if we depend on His will and not our will that will fail us sooner or later.

The Lord will work things out for our good, if we put our problems in His hands and leave them there, because our hands are weak and can drop things and break them into pieces.

The Lord will work things out for our good, if we believe that the Lord will follow through on supplying all of our needs that He knows so very well, even before we were born.

The Lord will work things out for our good, if we love and obey Him no matter what we go through in our lives because it is not too hard for the Lord to bless us on our good days and bad days.

The Lord will work things out for our good, if we confess and repent of our sins unto the Lord who can surely do anything but fail us, while we can mess things up in our own lives and regret it.

The Lord will work things out for our good, if we live our lives unto Him day after day and don't worry about anything that the Lord Jesus Christ can work out for our good.

Only You Can Control You

Only you can control your thoughts.

Only you can control your behavior.

Only you can control what you say.

Only you can control your mouth.

Only you can control your hands.

Only you can control your feet.

Only you can control your eyes.

Only you can control your feelings.

Only you can control your emotions.

Only you can control your actions.

God can't control you.

God gave you a free will to choose to control yourself or not choose to control yourself.

The devil can't control you.

The devil has no control over your free will to choose.

The devil can only tempt you to sin against God, who doesn't control anyone and make them love and obey Him.

Only you can control you.

No one can make you say something wrong.

No one can make you do something wrong.

The devil can't make you sin against God.

The devil can't control you and make you do evil.

Only you can control your life.

Only you can control your destiny.

Only you can control you and only you can choose to do right.

Only you can control you and choose to do wrong.

Only you can control what you eat.

Only you can control what you drink.

Only you can control you to love or hate.

Only you can control you to do good or evil.

In the Garden of Eden, the devil could not control Eve and make her eat the forbidden fruit.

In the Garden of Eden, Eve could not control Adam and make him eat the forbidden fruit.

Up in heaven, God did not control Lucifer and make him choose to rebel against Him.

God is not a controlling God.

God gave us all a free will to love Him or not love Him.

If God was a controlling God and had control over you and me, then God would not be love.

Only you can control you or not control you.

Only you can be out of control with your words and actions.

No one can control you and make you do anything that you don't want to do, even if he or she puts a gun to your head.

You can control you, even if your life is in danger because even that can't make you get out of control of yourself.

You can control you so you can die with dignity if you choose not to let anyone take that away from you.

No one can control you, who God didn't create to be controlled.

We True Children of God

We true children of God can't ignore the prejudices in this world like they don't exist.

We true children of God can't ignore the hatred in this world like it doesn't exist.

We true children of God can't ignore the crimes in this world like they don't exist.

We true children of God can't ignore the spiritualism in this world like it doesn't exist.

We true children of God can't ignore the injustices in this world like they don't exist.

We true children of God can't ignore the poverty in this world like it doesn't exist.

We true children of God can't live in a troubled world and stay all to ourselves when God appointed us to spread the gospel of his Son, Jesus Christ, to all the world.

We true children of God cannot stay shut in and stay away from this dying world, because many people need to hear about Jesus Christ and see Jesus in our daily lives.

We true children of God can't ignore that many people are lost and dying in their sins and pretend like sin doesn't exist.

We true children of God can't ignore the terrible times we are living in these last days.

We should not be comfortable in troubled times like they have no bad effect on us.

We true children of God can't ignore anyone turning their back on Jesus and leaving the church like it doesn't move our hearts.

We need to try to bring our brother or sister back in the church.

We true children of God can't ignore any kind of sin within our own hearts and pretend that the Lord will overlook it and let us get away with it.

We true children of God can't ignore anyone not being like Jesus Christ, because anyone in their own right mind can choose to confess and repent of their sins and live a renewed life unto Jesus Christ.

We true children of God can't ignore anyone's destiny and pretend there won't be hellfire and brimstone below the heavens one day when Jesus will destroy all who are lost in their sins.

Is Like

The news media is like a king sitting on his throne reporting a lot of bad news, like a cold war legacy.

Commercials on TV are nonstop, like eating food to live.

War is like a massive earthquake that doesn't care about killing thousands of people, regardless of their age or gender.

Crimes are like having no cure for cancer that is killing so many people.

Being overweight is like a toxic train wreck that is hard to clean up.

Working too much is like a dog throwing up vomit and licking it back up.

Being self-centered is like a wildfire burning up anything in its path.

Retirement is like a bubble that can burst and have no substance.

History is like a crown that needs to be polished up to wear.

Mental illness is like a heatwave scorching the grass.

The government is like an unstable man who doesn't have himself together.

This world is like a car accident causing a traffic jam.

Our lives are like the wind that blows in different directions, for only Jesus to know where it will end up.

Our destiny is like the unknown that only Jesus Christ truly knows and will not be surprised if we go with Him back to heaven when He comes back again or if we go to hell for holding onto even one known unrepented sin.

Having a relationship with Jesus is like heaven on earth in this wicked world where sin is like a poisonous snake that will bite us without any hesitation if we walk towards it like it is harmless.

Is No Better Than

A righteous man is no better than a wicked man, but a righteous man is completely different from a wicked man.

A righteous man is no better than a wicked man, but a righteous man knows what it means to pray to the Lord.

A righteous man is no better than a wicked man, but a righteous man knows what it means to wait on the Lord.

A righteous man is no better than a wicked man, but a righteous man knows what it means to trust the Lord.

A righteous man is no better than a wicked man, but a righteous man knows what it means to fear the Lord.

A righteous man is no better than a wicked man, but a righteous man knows what it means to be faithful unto the Lord.

A righteous man is no better than a wicked man, but a righteous man knows what it means to love the Lord.

A righteous man is no better than a wicked man, but a righteous man knows what it means to obey the Lord.

A righteous man is no better than a wicked man, but a righteous man knows what it means to live right unto the Lord.

A righteous man is no better than a wicked man, but they both belong to the Lord.

A righteous man is no better than a wicked man, but a righteous man will confess and repent of his sins unto the Lord.

A righteous man is no better than a wicked man, but a righteous man will go to heaven when Jesus comes back again.

A righteous man is no better than a wicked man, and they both will die and go to the grave.

A righteous man is no better than a wicked man, and they both have a free will.

A righteous man is no better than a wicked man, but a righteous man is completely different from a wicked man because a righteous man knows what it means to deny oneself and pick up one's cross to follow Jesus Christ.

If a righteous man's righteousness is like filthy rags before the Lord, then no wicked man can be right before the Lord, who will forgive a wicked man of his sins if he will confess, repent and turn from his wicked ways to live right unto the Lord.

To Truly Know Oneself

To truly know oneself is to know what you can do and what you can't do.

To truly know oneself is a good thing.

To truly know oneself can sometimes be a challenge.

To truly know oneself is not so easy to do.

To truly know oneself is a mature thing.

To truly know oneself means you can change your life for the better.

To truly know oneself means you can help someone else to get to know you.

To truly know oneself is a good experience.

To truly know oneself can surely help to get rid of being ignorant towards oneself.

To truly know oneself can surely help you and me be in control of oneself.

To truly know oneself is a blessing and not a curse.

To truly know oneself is to heal your soul.

To truly know oneself can surely keep you out of trouble.

To truly know oneself is strength in your character.

To truly know oneself is to know your strengths and weaknesses.

To truly know oneself is to know who you are.

To truly know oneself is knowing your own sins so you can confess and repent unto the Lord Jesus Christ.

To truly know oneself can give you a change of heart to deny self and let Jesus live in your heart because Jesus truly knows you better than you will ever know yourself.

The Bible Will Tell Us

The Bible will tell us how the sun began.

The Bible will tell us how the moon began.

The Bible will tell us how the stars began.

The Bible will tell us how the universe began.

The Bible will tell us how the birds and bees began.

The Bible will tell us how the animals began.

The Bible will tell us how the trees began.

The Bible will tell us how the rivers began.

The Bible will tell us how the oceans began.

The Bible will tell us how man began.

The Bible will tell us how woman began.

The Bible will tell us how children began.

The Bible will tell us how the angels began.

The Bible will tell us how the devil began.

The Bible will tell us how sin began.

The Bible will tell us how the heavens began.

The Bible will tell us how the earth began.

No one can tell us that anything else began outside of the Bible.

Nothing else exists outside of the Bible.

The Bible tells us that God is the beginning and the end.

The Bible tells us that God's Son, Jesus Christ, is the creator of all things.

The Bible tells us how other worlds began.

The Bible tells us how the day began.

The Bible tells us how the night began.

The Bible tells us how nature began.

The Bible tells us how marriage began.

The Bible tells us how life began.

The Bible tells us how death began.

The Bible tells us how all creatures began.

The Bible tells us how time began.

The Bible tells us how prophecy began.

The Bible tells us how the truth began.

The Bible tells us how lies began.

The Bible tells us how beauty began.

The Bible tells us how victory began.

The Bible tells us how food began.

The Bible tells us how our breath that we breathe began.

The Bible tells us how wisdom began.

The Bible tells us how love began.

The Bible tells us how foolishness began.

The Bible tells us how jealousy began.

The Bible tells us how worship began.

The Bible tells us how knowledge began.

The Bible tells us how perfection began.

The Bible tells us how laws began.

The Bible doesn't tell us how God began.

We all would be vanished from existence before we knew how God began.

The Bride of Jesus Christ

The bride of Jesus Christ will not give in to worldly fashions.

The bride of Jesus Christ will dress in modest apparel.

The bride of Jesus Christ will submit her will to Jesus.

The bride of Jesus Christ will stay very close by her husband Jesus.

The bride of Jesus Christ will never disrespect her husband Jesus.

The bride of Jesus Christ will have many spiritual children by Jesus.

The bride of Jesus Christ will work to win souls to Jesus.

The bride of Jesus Christ will set the right example for the people of the world.

The bride of Jesus Christ will be faithful to her husband Jesus.

The bride of Jesus Christ is more beautiful than any woman.

The bride of Jesus Christ is more loving than any mother to her children.

The bride of Jesus Christ is more trustworthy to her husband Jesus than any wife to her husband.

The bride of Jesus Christ will always know that her husband Jesus will catch her if she falls.

The bride of Jesus Christ will always let her husband Jesus lead her on the straight and narrow road.

The bride of Jesus Christ will never change on her husband Jesus, who she loves and obeys every day because Jesus loves her and will give her a heavenly crown when He comes back again to take His church bride to heaven.

The bride of Jesus Christ is the most beautiful, loyal, humble and most wise queen that this world will ever have.

The bride of Jesus Christ will never try to rule over her husband Jesus.

The bride of Jesus Christ is His true and one and only church, because Jesus has only one church bride to take to heaven.

Jesus is only married to His church bride and not to the people of the world.

Anyone can choose to repent of their sins and live a renewed life unto Jesus and be His bride and win lost souls for all the angels in heaven to rejoice over.

We Can Only Truly Make it Through Jesus

We can only truly make it through Jesus, not through zodiac signs that can't keep married couples together for life like Jesus does.

We can only truly make it through Jesus, not through luck that can't protect us from harm and danger like Jesus does.

We can only truly make it through Jesus, not through magic that can't work things out in our lives like Jesus does.

We can only make it through Jesus, not through money that can't heal our minds, bodies, and souls like Jesus does.

We can only make it through Jesus, not through our own will that can't supply all of our needs like Jesus does.

We can only truly make it through Jesus, not through our feelings that can't always be sure to be right like Jesus.

We can only truly make it through Jesus, not through our lives that can't give us health and strength like Jesus does.

We can only make it through Jesus, not through our education that can't make us wise like Jesus does.

We can only truly make it through Jesus, not through ourselves who can't see all things, hear all things and can't do all things like Jesus does.

We can only truly make it through Jesus, not through this world that can't pour out blessings upon you and me like Jesus does.

Salvation

Salvation is not in being a pope in the church.

Salvation is not in being an elder in the church.

Salvation is not in being a deacon in the church.

Salvation is not in being an usher in the church.

Salvation is not in being a musician in the church.

Salvation is not in being a singer in the church.

Salvation is not in being a men's ministry leader in the church.

Salvation is not in being a women's ministry leader in the church.

Salvation is not in being a treasurer in the church.

Salvation is not in being a clerk in the church.

Salvation is not in being a community service leader in the church.

Salvation is not in being an evangelist in the church.

Salvation is not in having spiritual gifts in the church.

Salvation is not in being a counselor in the church.

Salvation is only in Jesus Christ, who can save us from our sins.

Salvation is not in being a vegetarian.

Salvation is not in being a youth ministry leader.

Salvation is not in being a 50+ ministry leader.

Salvation is not in being a prayer warrior.

Salvation is not in being a righteous man.

Salvation is not in being a righteous woman.

Salvation is not in being a community service worker.

Salvation is not in being a church member.

Salvation is not in being a Bible school teacher.

Salvation is not in being a tithes and offerings giver in the church.

Salvation is only in Jesus Christ, who is our Lord and Savior.

Salvation is not in our good works in the church.

Salvation is only in believing in Jesus Christ.

The devil can preach in the church.

The devil can hold positions in the church.

The devil can pretend to do good works in the church, but the devil doesn't believe in Jesus Christ.

The devil has his human agents in the church who don't believe Jesus Christ is our only salvation.

Even though the devil has his human agents in the church, Jesus Christ is the head of the church and will separate the wheat from the tares.

Jesus Christ is the head of the church who will save us from our sins.

Jesus Christ is the head of the church who will give us His salvation of saving grace.

Salvation is not in the government.

Salvation is not in the White House.

Salvation is not in talents.

Salvation is not in money.

Salvation is not in horoscopes.

Salvation is not in skills.

Salvation is not in mediums and psychics.

Salvation is not in a job.

Salvation is not in a career.

Salvation is not in wealth.

Salvation is only in Jesus Christ, who can save anyone from being lost in sin if they confess and repent and live their lives unto Him.

Salvation is not in evolution.

Salvation is not in success.

Salvation is not in fame.

Salvation is not in achievements.

Salvation is not in athletics.

Salvation is not in sports.

Salvation is not in being beautiful.

Salvation is not in food.

Salvation is not in being a hero.

Salvation is not in having trophies.

Salvation is not in being a genius.

Salvation is only in Jesus Christ, who is worthy to save us from our sins when no one else and nothing else is worthy to save us from our sins.

Salvation is not in education.

Salvation is not in science.

Salvation is not in nature.

Salvation is not in movie stars.

Salvation is not in entertainers.

Salvation is not in astronauts.

Salvation is not in any angel.

Salvation is not in any creature.

Salvation is only in Jesus Christ, not anyone else in heaven and on earth.

Salvation is not in any doctor.

Salvation is not in any surgeon.

Salvation is not in any judge.

Salvation is not in any president.

Salvation is not in any profit.

Salvation is not in any military.

Salvation is only in Jesus Christ, who can save us from our sins.

Salvation is not in any witchdoctor.

Salvation is not in luck.

Salvation is not in any animal.

Salvation is not in a deep dream.

Salvation is not in spiritualism.

Salvation is not in anyone in this world.

Salvation is not in anything in this world.

Salvation is only in Jesus Christ, who is the one and only One who can save us from our sins if we believe in Him to be saved.